# Women's Ideal Liberation

*Islamic Versus Western Understanding*

## التحرير المثالي للمرأة

مقارنة بين المفهوم الإسلامي والمفهوم الغربي

### Rukaiyah (Laurel) Hill Abdulsalam

**All rights reserved.** No part of this publication may be reproduced, translated, stored in a retrieval system or transmitted in any form or by any means – electronic, mechanical, photocopying, recording or otherwise – without written permission from the Author. This includes the scanning, uploading, forwarding and free distribution of its contents via the internet. If you've obtained an electronic copy without paying for it, please replace it by purchasing a licensed e-book as indicated on our website.

© **Rukaiyah (Laurel) Hill Abdulsalam; printed with permission by Dar Abul-Qasim (authorized distributor), 2012**
**2nd edition, 2nd printing; in print since 1998**

*King Fahd National Library Cataloging-in-Publication Data*
Abdulsalam, Rukaiyah (Laurel) Hill
 Women's Ideal Liberation: Islamic Versus Western Understanding/
 Rukiyah (Laurel) Hill Abdulsalam - 2 - Jeddah, 2012
 162 p., 14 x 21 cm
 ISBN 978-9960-887-52-4
 1 – Women in Islam   2 – Muslim women –Europe
 I – Title
 219.1dc      1433/6706

Legal Deposit no. 1433/6706
ISBN: 978-9960-887-52-4

**DAR ABUL-QASIM**
PO Box 6156
Jeddah 21442, Saudi Arabia

Telephone (966-2) 671-4793
Fax (966-2) 672-5523

e-mail: abulqasimbooks@hotmail.com
website: www.abulqasimbooks.com

THIS BOOK HAS BEEN PRODUCED IN COLLABORATION WITH
**SAHEEH INTERNATIONAL™**
*Professional Editing and Typesetting of Islamic Literature*
www.saheehinternational.com

# Table of Contents

Foreword .................................................................................. i
Acknowledgment .................................................................. iv

Manmade System – The Drama ............................................ 1
    Women's Inequality Throughout History ..................... 2
    Obviously Designed by a Man ......................................... 5
    Morality Defined ................................................................ 8
    The Abolishment of the Family ....................................... 9
    Oppression Unveiled ....................................................... 15

Women and the Work Force ................................................. 20
    Out of the Home and into the Work Force ................. 24
    How the System Stigmatizes the Mother ..................... 27
    The Force That Is Negligent ........................................... 29
    Birth of the Super Woman – Necessity, Not Choice .... 30
    Gender Discrimination ................................................... 33

The Media .............................................................................. 35
    The Mighty Media .......................................................... 35
    Media Portrayal of the Islamic World ......................... 38
    Western Scholars and Islam ........................................... 39
    Prince Charles at the Oxford Centre for Islamic Studies .. 41
    The Negative Portrayal and Media Bloopers ............... 45
    Gains and Setbacks ......................................................... 46

Life Without God .................................................................. 51
    The Impact of Civilization Without Culture ............... 51
    Morality Comes Only from Religion ........................... 54
    Man Is Unable to Guide Himself ................................... 57
    The Jahiliyyah Society .................................................... 59
    The Prophet of Islam ...................................................... 61
    Islam Freed the Pagans ................................................... 63

We Are Equal, but We Are Not the Same .......................... 66
  Towards Androgyny ..................................................... 66
  Islam – The Key to Human Liberation ........................ 70
  Islam – Empowerment to Be One's True Self ............. 73
  Western Degradation of the Woman ........................... 76
  Sex Objects, Immorality, and Rampant Divorce .......... 78

Freedom to Be Undressed ..................................................... 81
  In the West: Oppressed If You Are Dressed ............... 81
  What Is Beneath the Veil? ........................................... 84
  The Hijab Fits Women's Nature .................................. 87
  The Islamic Culture ..................................................... 90

The Segregated Society ........................................................ 94
  Casual Relations Lead to Casualties ............................ 94
  Education for Women and Men ................................... 96
  The Coed Facility and Man's Paradise ........................ 97
  Academic Sexual Harassment .................................... 100
  A Woman's Right to Peace and Justice ..................... 101

Moral Liberation of the Western Woman ........................... 104
  Redefining Abortion .................................................. 111
  Vocations for Women ................................................ 113
  Cosmetic Surgery for the Sake of Approval .............. 115
  From Silicone Implants to Silicone Bottles ............... 118
  Family Needs a Mother ............................................. 119
  Progress and Civilization ........................................... 122

The Significance of Marriage and Child Care .................... 125
  Islam's Preservation of the Individual, Marriage
     and Society ............................................................. 126
  Building Nations ........................................................ 128

The Marriage Proposal ..................................................... 131
    Women in Islam .......................................................... 131
    Companionship ........................................................... 136
    Leadership .................................................................. 138

Who Is Liberated in the West? ........................................ 140
    Is Paradise for Men Only? ......................................... 140
    Divorce in the West .................................................... 141
    Children Without Fathers ........................................... 142
    Divorce in Islam ......................................................... 144

Conclusion ....................................................................... 149
Bibliography .................................................................... 150

# Foreword

*Women's Ideal Liberation* is a comparison of Western culture and its women with Islamic culture and Muslim women. Comprised of current statistics, documentation and analysis, the trends of Western society are outlined in considerable detail in order to show how Islam guides individuals and societies clear from the many problems created out of ignorance and blind reliance on manmade laws. Western culture is considered a manmade system due to its non-adherence to any one religion. The vast differences between the West and Islam (including lifestyles, the concept of family life, marriage, motherhood, education, the workplace, public interaction, women's status, and marriage and divorce practices) are discussed in light of Western laws and of *shari'ah* (Islamic law), which is based upon the Qur'an[1] and *hadith*.[2]

Before any culture, way of life or religion can be appreciated, one must first understand that every person is a product of his own upbringing, culture and society. As mechanical as that might sound, most of what one believes and how he lives is due to socialization. Sociologists point out that people assimilate their culture without much hesitation when they are young. Each person is apt to feel that his own culture is superior because that notion makes him feel secure. However, once one begins to question why he does things, he will come to understand himself and the many aspects of life.

The inquisitive mind is one that takes time to think, reflect and desires knowledge. Notice how small children are curious about their surroundings and eager to learn about

---

[1] The final revelation from Allah to mankind.
[2] Sayings of Prophet Muhammad (ﷺ). (Note: The Arabic symbol which appears after Prophet Muhammad's name throughout this text stands for "blessings and peace be upon him.")

everything around them. To be liberated one should free himself to seek the truths reflected in science, in nature, within the self, and, more importantly, the truth found in religion. An open-minded person is not afraid to look beyond his limited position in life and believes that other religions and ways of life are worth being studied.

Conscientious people living in the Western world have many values which are Islamic. They strongly believe in work ethic, self-sufficiency, freedom, respect, and deploring oppression, which are also Islamic values. But even with these shared values, many Westerners know very little about Islam. Only until I met a Muslim who was willing to talk about religion did I find the missing pieces I had been searching for.

Finally, my quest for religion was fulfilled – after a decade of searching, after affiliation with Christianity, and after the study of other religions – I had been given the answer. The initial thought that struck me upon finding Islam was, "Why had I not learned about Islam during my years of education or within my culture?" From my schooling I recall only a brief mention of the Islamic empire and Islamic art, and that was the extent of it.

When I began to seriously study Islam, I realized I had found something very valuable. I wanted to share my discovery that had been denied me my whole life. Because of my upbringing in a non-Islamic country, I am familiar with the myths and half-truths propagated by Western society which guarantee people's continued enslavement to their own desires. Now I realize why I had never heard about Islam and why there were very few books available in my country.

The aim of this work is to show how Western[3] women, far from being liberated, are only lead to believe so. From

---

[3]The word "Western" is used throughout this text to refer to the European-American ideology, largely materialistic and non-religious, which has become a dominant influence in the modern world.

an Islamic perspective it is easy to see the destructive paths they follow. It is true oppression that keeps them powerless and confused, bound by and for the benefit of a manmade system. This book is for anyone willing to be jostled out of complacency and lethargic acceptance of the tides and trends of pop-culture and those social norms which too often sabotage the inner desire to fulfill one's self in an appropriate way. It is a forthright attempt to banish the egocentric way of thinking which destroys one's ability to seek answers with an open mind.

My intention is also to clarify the true definition of "liberation" in Islamic terms. When the human being acknowledges that freedom begins with complete submission to God (Allah in Arabic), then true liberation can be experienced. All systems for enlarging, perfecting and allowing the self to flower will eventually fail – except for Islam. It is my ardent wish to point out to women that there exists a way of life that preserves, protects, comforts, dignifies and liberates her (and her male counterpart) from the snares of manmade ideologies. That way of life is the sole worship of One Deity, One God, who is Allah (Glorified and Exalted is He), and adherence to His religion, Islam.

Rukaiyah (Laurel) Hill Abdulsalam<br>
July, 1998[4]<br>
Jeddah, Saudi Arabia

---

[4]Even though the data gathered in 1998 for the 1st edition may now seem "outdated" for this subsequent reprint, the information is still relevant. In actual fact, many of the situations are regrettably worse fifteen years later.

# Acknowledgment

I wish to thank my husband, Professor Mohammed Abdulsalam, for the constant encouragement he gave me. His professional and generous input was inspirational and often led to many hours of brainstorming. He was never too busy to lend an ear, yet one of the busiest people I've ever known.

Next, I want to give credit to two other special people in my life. The first one is my mother, whose contributions began a long time ago when, as her child, she instilled in me some of the most vital and unchanging values (which have proven to be Islamic principles) – they have remained steadfast and true: for where there is endurance, there is truth; and where there is truth, there is Islam. The second person is my mother-in-law, who played a major role in this work by acting as a "surrogate mother" to our two-year old son (not an easy task) during various phases of this project – most importantly, while I was abroad for four consecutive months completing the final draft.

Finally, I want to thank Dar Abul-Qasim and the Saheeh International editing staff.

*May our reward be found with Allah.*

# Manmade System - The Drama

It has been claimed that life is a stage. If this is true, then the star of life's drama is woman. Nowadays, the words "liberated" and "liberation" have completely lost their true meanings. Instead of describing one's freedom from tyranny, oppression or manmade systems, they have come to mean being free from prohibitions – being free to do and to live however one wants. Confusion about the true meanings of these important words is heard more and more from women because they are terms with which women identify. A result of this confusion is that Western women are unable to see the reality of their own oppression. People are using other words flagrantly and incorrectly too. Words are taken out of context to alter their meanings – words such as "oppression" and "human rights." What is evident is that these terms have been redefined under the context of the liberalized, modern society. The word "oppression" is defined as "that which oppresses or burdens, a feeling of being heavily weighed down, either mentally or physically; depression, weariness."[5] "Oppress" means "to subjugate or persecute by unjust or tyrannical use of force or authority."[6] But nowadays, many Westerners use this word to mean anything that infringes on their personal freedom, even if the infringement is a law or regulation which might protect them.

For them oppression is a Muslim woman who covers all of her body. Firstly, the Muslim woman dresses this way because it is a command from her Creator. Secondly, adherence to divine laws protects the believer both in this life and the life to come. By properly covering her body, the Muslim woman is viewed with dignity and respect and is not seen as an object to be preyed upon. Indeed, the Muslim woman regards Western women with pity. Skyrocketing

---

[5]*American Heritage Dictionary of the English Language*, p. 922.
[6]Ibid., p. 922.

rape statistics, sexual harassment lawsuits, a burgeoning female pornography industry, AIDS... the woman who is suffering oppression is not the Muslim but her Western counterpart.

People have grown to believe that if they are granted more freedom, they will be happier. Consequently, they no longer feel a personal responsibility to society or even to one another, much less themselves. This is only the beginning of the drama. The curtain rises...

## Women's Inequality Throughout History

Although Islam granted women equal status with men fourteen hundred years ago, equality for women throughout history and throughout most parts of the world has always been a hotly debated topic. Historically, women have been abused, mistreated and certainly misrepresented. Even the most widely accepted world religions stigmatized, demeaned and stripped women of their human rights and denied them their personality. Their status in relation to men was never defined. Dr. Jamal Badawi's essay, *The Status of Woman in Islam*, points out very distinct legal practices which historically kept women in subjection to men:

> In India the subjection of women was the first principle rule and intent of the law. They were denied any kind of financial independence. They were not entitled to inheritance, as this was reserved only for the males of the family. And according to Hindu scriptures, the lives of women were not any more promising. For a woman to be considered a good woman or wife, her character had to be entirely willing to be dominated by her male relations, especially her husband. Her physical, emotional and mental capacities were strictly regulated and in control of her husband. Further, in Athens, women were considered as

juveniles who were in need of a guardian throughout her lifetime. Their guardians were, of course, the males of their family and then their husbands upon marriage. The woman's consent with regards to her marriage partner was not necessary, and she was traditionally brought up to accept whoever her parents chose as her future mate. In Rome women were also considered as juveniles or "babes" and "wards," or better stated, as a gender who needed assistance at every turn. According to men, they were incapable of performing any actions of their own accord. They lived within the confines of their husbands, as wives. The Encyclopedia Britannica summarized the lawful implications of the Roman civilization and women as those entirely in need of dependence. When they married, all of their personal property became the absolute property of their husbands. Their status was akin to a slave's. They had absolutely no civil liberties and no rights within the public domain. Contractual matters were out of their control. In Scandinavia, as late as the Code of Christian V at the end of the 17th century, it was dictated that if a woman married without the consent of her tutor, then he could act as administrator during her life. According to English Common Law, all real property which a wife held at the time of a marriage became the possession of her husband. He was entitled to the rent from her land and to any profit which might be made from operating the estate during the joint life of the spouses. As to the wife's personal property, the husband's power was complete. He had the right to spend it as he saw fit. As this might sound unbelievably oppressive and gloomy, by the late 19th century, women's status gained some ground. They were allowed to own property by the Married Women's Property Acts in 1870 and then re-amended in 1882. During this same period Sir Henry Maine wrote: "No society which preserves any tincture of Christian institutions is likely to restore to married women the personal liberty conferred on them by the Middle Roman Law." John Stuart Mill wrote: "We are continually told that civilization and Christianity have restored to the woman her just rights. Meanwhile, the wife is the actual bondservant of her husband; no less so, as far as the legal obligation goes, than slaves commonly so called." In order to expound upon this thought, under Mosaic law a woman was "betrothed." This meant in no lesser terms that she was bought and was therefore a piece of property. She was the possession of her husband. She had no legal rights to agree to marriage, and she had no rights to divorce: all of these rights were in the possession of her husband. He had all legal authority and all rights to all decisions.[7]

In the book *Marriage East and West,* David and Vera Mace share an even more interesting summarization along these themes:

> Let no one suppose, either, that our Christian heritage is free of such slighting judgments. It would be hard to find anywhere a collection of more degrading references to the female sex than the early Church Fathers provide... in a portion of the writing of the Fathers... woman was represented as the door of Hell, as the mother of all human ills... She could live in continual

---

[7]*The Status of Woman in Islam*, excerpts and information from pp. 6-9.

penance on account of the curses she has brought upon the world... She should be ashamed of her dress, for it is the memorial of her fall. She should be especially ashamed of her beauty, for it is the most potent instrument of the devil. One of the most scathing of these attacks on woman is that of Tertullian: "Do you know that you are each an Eve? The sentence of God on this sex of yours lives in this age: the guilt must of necessity live too. You are the devil's gateway: you are the unsealer of that forbidden tree; you are the first deserters of the divine law; you are she who persuades him whom the devil was not valiant enough to attack. You destroyed so easily God's image, man..."[8]

From the very conception of their history and lineage, Western civilizations comprised from early Christian theology were incapable of granting women rights. However, as time went on, women became more enlightened. They began fighting for equality and equal opportunity, not under any religious banner (certainly not Christianity) but through their human inner conviction (*fitrah*) which told them they were as valuable as men and not evil. Women finally gained some ground, but only after much struggle. First, they had to gain rights to equal education. Next, they had to prove their intelligence through their successes with higher education.

## **Obviously Designed by a Man**

Western society prides itself for being the land of liberty and incessantly boasts that it is a place which grants people freedom. It certainly does not inflict many religious or moral values on its citizens, but that, in itself, is not

---

[8] Ibid., p. 10.

necessarily good. In fact, the American system does not have an identifying religion at all. So from where does it or its citizens derive their ideas of morality? How are the laws of the land defined and laid out? Does it gather ideas from all the world religions? If so, this is contrary to sound religious conviction, for certainly, what one religion may call moral another may call immoral. Under this pretext how do Western systems come up with moral guidelines?

The West cannot derive its laws or moral standards from one religion because then it would be forcing a religion on its people. This runs counter to the right of freedom of religion and separation of church and state. It is of great irony that many American citizens claim that the nation was founded under the Christian religion. And it is highly doubtful when a few points are taken into consideration. Firstly, America has inflicted usury on its people, which, according to the Bible, is immoral. Secondly, the legalization of prostitution and gambling and the sale and prolific use of alcohol and pornography runs counter to most religious values – certainly those of Christendom.

Instead of following religion, Western civilization did what it had to – created its own manmade systems through trial and error. According to Western philosophy, trends, and the colossal crime rate, very little seems to be considered immoral anymore. The West's manmade systems have made life more difficult because they have changed several of life's essential components (economy, justice, education, social control, family life, work environment, etc.) by stipulating their own values, laws and regulations for each one. Instead of treating life as a whole, the system has addressed life by bits and pieces. From this, man's inept ability to see life from a broad, clear perspective is apparent. In reality, life cannot be divided into separate parts because every component has an impact on the others. For example, if the school system fails, children grow up to be illiterate. If children grow up to be illiterate, the society is intellectually weakened. If the society is weakened, the family structure is threatened. Life is indivisible. The domino theory reflects this premise – if one domino falls, then all the dominoes feel the impact and fall down. Subsequently, any attempts to impose different values and rules to life's many components cause confusion and ultimately destroy the cohesiveness needed for balanced human life filled with peace and dignity. It is like being tossed to and fro in a stormy sea with waves threatening to pull one under at any moment.

Although there is a degree of social order in America, it possesses the highest crime rate in the world, and it has numerous other social and economic problems. An example of how this manmade system does not work for individuals can be seen in some staggering statistics. The number of jobs that paid poverty-level wages between 1979 and 1984 was 44%. The chance an individual American will experience poverty through a ten year period is one in four. The percentage of poor who are white in America is 68%, black 28% and Hispanic 13%. The percentage of families without fathers who did not receive child support payments in 1985 was 60%. The median weekly child support payment received per child in 1986 was $16.00. And lastly, a Harvard University study's estimation of the homeless population in 1988 was 350,000.[9] These statistics have not improved, and, in fact, have gotten worse all around due to the economic deficit and poor economic status of the United States. According to news reports as of 1995, the national budget deficit in America was at an all time high of four trillion dollars.

---

[9]*U.S. News & World Report,* U.S. News Education Program America's Homeless, Poor and Homeless in America: A Data Base, 1988.

## Morality Defined

From these revealing statistics, hopefully one thing has been realized: degenerate man finds it difficult to make moral decisions. If degenerate man makes a society, he will say that drinking alcohol is moral, having premarital sex is moral, and that posing in pornographic magazines is also okay. Therefore, morality as a principle does not exist without religion, where manmade morality does. In other words, there are people who think they are religious, but they act like materialists. They have been taught to tell the truth, not to steal, and that to kill is a sin, but they have not learned nor do they practice the religion from where these values were derived. Therefore, they remain uncommitted to religion. In this way they are divided between the spiritual and the material and do not make the final step towards full morality. When such an individual or group of people continue to believe in the morals but do not believe in the religion from which those morals came, then it is possible to have virtuous atheists, agnostics and wandering seekers of some brand of truth.

Modern cultures are replacing religious morality with social control and discipline. In this way the system only tries to satisfy and control the masses. Although this may work for the society, it does not fulfill the human being. Human beings are born with an inner need for worship and guidance. If they get caught halfway between spirituality and materialism, they become lost. They tend to think in terms of immediacy and not the long term plan: the Hereafter, eternity, Heaven and Hell. Materialists say, "Why shouldn't I live as I please or live for the moment?" The pervasive availability and production of pornography and liberal attitudes of the day are symptomatic of this type of philosophy. Modern-day feminists are also an example of people who want less morality (or less religion) because they continue to ask for more unlimited rights which debase their true natures.

So not surprisingly, social control has replaced religion. The system has cleverly traded in the calling to all mankind to seek God and has substituted this higher calling for a lesser one, patriotism. In this, the religious person finds great struggle and conflict. For example, constitutional rights which are supposed to guarantee people "freedom of religion" might literally be interpreted to mean that people are now "freed from religion." Freedom of religion has been whittled down, restricted, and manipulated by limitations and legal enforcement designed to keep the masses faithful to the system. The basic fundamental human right is to worship God first, but it has been replaced with the manmade agenda to serve country first. Western culture claims to have been founded under the banner of Christianity (because the founding fathers who signed the Declaration of Independence were said to be "godly" men), but one is hard pressed to find within its manmade system anything relating to following God's way besides its monetary system which uses the words "In God we trust."

## **The Abolishment of the Family**

The current chaos in Western society is felt by women and children most because the manmade system has neglected their needs and rights. When religion is not placed at the center of importance of a society, then for every step towards progress means a step away from religion and family.[10] Contrary to this, true religious guidance has always stressed the importance of family, women, and especially of mothers.[11] In the West other areas of life often take priority, with the family unit sometimes ranking last.

---

[10]*Islam Between East and West,* p. 175.
[11]Ibid., p. 179.

According to most politicians, the family and mother are not the basic cornerstone of the society, and according to many individuals, work is more important than family. At once, this has stripped women of their basic human right to procreate and has tried to alter woman's identity as the significant "other" in the scope of human life (as if babies can grow up without a mother's love). At the same time it has forced young children into situations in which they are unable to find security, love and real care. Can life go on without the woman being willing to bear future generations? Apparently, some people feel it can. Can families remain strong and united if the job and money have become more important than the individuals of a family? Can children grow up under these conditions and become emotionally secure and confident individuals? Additionally, women in the West are still oppressed in the marriage custom, and they are being underpaid in the workplace. In either situation, women are the victims.

Friedrich Engels, a German of Jewish descent and one of the founders of present-day Communist theory, openly supports the breakdown of the family unit:

> "It will become clear that for the liberation of women, the first condition is to introduce again all women into public activity, and that means the abolition of the isolated family as a socioeconomic unit... The care and education of children becomes a public affair; society looks after all children alike, whether they are legitimate or not."[12]

Likewise, Marx said, "The abolition [i.e., dying out] of the family means the socialization of man..."[13] Hence, mother is replaced by daycare, parents are replaced by education, and

---
[12]Ibid., p. 176.
[13]Ibid., p. 176.

belonging to family becomes belonging to society. For socialization to take root, the advantages of family, motherhood, and the maternal instinct must be uprooted and torn out of the human mind – especially out of the female psyche. In the West this process began several decades ago, and today it is nearing full realization. If anyone doubts this, then explain why there are so many social services on the American continent. On just two pages of the telephone directory for a small rural town in Pennsylvania was a long social service list for alcohol treatment programs, child abuse centers, drug and other substance abuse centers, a runaway switch board, a coalition against domestic violence and rape, an abortion hot line, pregnancy loss support programs, mental health support centers, sexual assault rehabilitation centers, a civil liberties union, and venereal disease information centers. After observing this, one can ask, "What has happened to people's lives, to the family, and to the important relations between the sexes?"

It can be concluded that in the West the relevance of the family and motherhood was sabotaged long ago. It began in subtle ways with innocent and cleverly sent messages which targeted women's minds. The media told them that being a wife and mother is oppressive and limiting and that children can raise themselves. It continued to akin children to rug rats and implied that raising children in nurseries is not harmful. Staying home with children was considered a waste of one's time and effort.

The signs of how civilization has degraded the mother are all around. The number of marriages is decreasing, while the number of divorces is escalating. The number of children per family is less, and the number of illegitimate children is on the rise. More women are being employed, and there are more single parent families. In 1975, the largest number of working women worldwide was in the Soviet Union, where eighty-two out of one hundred women were employed. During this period in history, the Soviet Union and America had the same and highest number of illegitimate children.[14]

Islam always put the family as the most important element of man's existence. It is suppose to be where one finds comfort and companionship and where the beauty of procreation through the lives of one's own children unfolds before his eyes. According to Islam, the woman, as mother, is a builder of nations. But today, in most parts of the world, mothers have been replaced by the public education system and daycare centers. People other than the family members are taking care of the children.

The morals of Western society have been dispersed. The values people blindly cling to are a series of mixed messages and contradictions. For example, in Western culture where pornography is a legal multimillion dollar empire, it is no longer considered wrong or exploitative. The "new wave thinking" is that the posing of nude women is okay because they are consenting adults. Similar to this but somewhat more confusing is the legalization and authorized approval of prostitution. However, it is presently legalized in only one state. What explains this obvious restriction and governmental control? If it is morally wrong or a threat to society, then why make it legal at all? This is similar to the "Don't tell" policy for homosexuals who want to enter the military: as long as it's kept quiet, it's okay. If morality is defined as that which is between two consenting adults, how is the restriction on prostitution or the prohibition of certain sexual acts between legally married people explained? Are not these acts between consenting adults?

Even more confusion is heard when feminists and others get on the ban wagon against beauty pageants, which have been in existence for seventy-five years (the same

---

[14]Ibid., pp. 177-178.

number of years women in this country were granted the right to vote). Beauty pageants promote the value of being beautiful. The contestants wear bathing suits and are judged greatly upon their beauty. (One must be at least pretty to even get into a pageant.) Has there ever been an ugly "beauty queen?"

What about other areas of society that no one seems bothered by, such as women casually going poolside wearing a next-to-nothing G-string bikini? What about topless bars and nude dance clubs? What about the models in the modeling industry? Are they not valued for their good looks? If concern about the exploitation of women is sincere, then the entire culture must come under scrutiny.

Where once a mother nurtured her children under the guidance of her religious values, daycare and the public education system now foster them through governmentally controlled programs in order to shape them into being good citizens. This can be described as nothing less than the move towards the dehumanization and despiritualization of man. Reverting back to Russia provides a good example. From the moment a Russian is born, he is taken from the hospital maternity ward to still more structured facilities like boarding schools. Just as cattle being driven from one plain to the next, he is led through a systematic process of dehumanization and drill only to end up at yet another structured setting.[15] To the former Russians, life was never equated with the comfort of home, family closeness, or the mother's presence.

Women have been greatly affected by the path Western civilization has taken them. Especially beautiful women – they are no longer human beings but rather toys to look at, admire and use. As objects of desire, men value women mostly in terms of sexual conquest and gratification. The

---

[15]Ibid., p. 179.

beautiful actress, the super model, or the victim of date rape on college campuses or on the battlefield are no longer human beings with feelings. They are instead a means of momentary fulfillment, visual delight and nothing more than a beautiful creature strolling down the public sidewalk or fashion runway. If women can be successfully stripped of their human identity, dignity and self-respect, then they can be more easily abused and manipulated. If their modesty and sense of morality can be diminished, they are easier targets to molest and sexually assault.

It must be noted that most of the institutions that objectify women as playthings would be out of business if women woke up and saw the light. Beauty pageants, modeling agencies, female pornography purveyors, and prostitution rings thrive because of the willing participation of women blinded by the myths fed them by this culture. It is distressing to see the semi-clothed female body increasingly splashed on billboards and in magazines selling everything from lipstick to batteries. And it is not as if all this freedom does not come with a high price tag. Female suicide, depression, and substance abuse are worldwide problems. What is wrong with this picture of "liberation?"

Certain realities are impossible to deny and must be faced. These mixed, hurt feelings are easily stirred in women today. Frustrations and disappointments can be seen and heard from the blue collar worker to the woman who holds the highest degree. Many are unfulfilled, overworked and lost. The epitome of the Western woman can be seen in an illustration of a woman who has a scientific doctorate degree and is working at one of the top academic universities in the United States. She is married and has children, but she is not happy. She faces discrimination and unfair treatment just because she is a woman. Although she has worked as hard as her male counterpart, she is never treated with the same level of respect. Her children miss her because she spends long hours at work. She and her husband have their own professional careers, and their relationship is practically non-existent. She is lonely and overworked. She asks herself, "What has my education gotten me?" and confides her feelings only to a few strangers because they are non-threatening. Her tears easily flow. She feels a rage buried deep inside her, as though she is going to explode one day. She worked so hard at her work that she miscarried a child, but "Nobody really cared," she said. Even the doctor coldly remarked, "I see no viable fetus" and left the room. She continued, "Everyone here expects you to get back in the saddle. No one has time to care about other people."

Many people seem to be drowning in life's sea of confusion, engulfed by waves at every turn crashing in on them. But it is the woman who is endlessly waiting for an outstretched hand. Numbed by the cold, harsh realities that keep smashing in upon her, she feels powerless over the force that incessantly pulls her down. But she is not powerless, weak or helpless. She only needs a guiding hand.

## **Oppression Unveiled**

Currently in the West there is an undeniable resurgence of women's advocates and feminists. Women are writing books such as, *Backlash – The Undeclared War Against American Women, Female Sexual Slavery,* and *The New Victorians – A Young Woman's Challenge to the Old Feminist Order.* Some of these are college texts used at American universities for women's studies. Today, there are numerous books exposing how Western women are being physically, sexually and emotionally assaulted. These books further show how desperately Western women are seeking a cure, not just a temporary fix. Although the problems of manmade systems are not new, it is clear there is an escalation regarding the degradation of women in Western cultures. The books being written about women's problems are invaluable because their message might stir in some women a sense of awareness as to what is happening. Many Western women are numbed by their years of abuse, and others are too busy to reflect on their situation. Older women tend to be in denial. They have learned to go through life trying not to feel, because when they do, it hurts too much.

There are, however, some enlightened women who have taken a greater interest in women's issues. Even though their minds are filled with knowledge and they see the reality of oppression, most women's advocates are void of real spiritual thought. They have no moral solutions to offer for the problems in their society, and why should they be expected to? After all, they are products of the manmade system, which is not an advocate of religion or morality. If these women advocates began to explore the concept of religious values, they would become more frustrated with the present system, realizing what it really promotes.

So what has been the result of these advocate's work? An undeclared war against men, attempting to "correct" the situation by becoming like men, i.e., "equal" to them. It is ironic that although many women do not want to identify themselves with feminism for fear of being labeled a feminazi or lesbian, most women still pattern their lives in a way which reflects what feminists uphold. This is a vital part of the drama. On one hand, Western women are drilled by the feminists, the media, the education system, and their political leaders who tell them they are the most liberated women on the face of the earth. Some women really believe this, but not entirely. On the other hand, women who are more honest about the situation know through their experiences with family, men, marriage, divorce and the educational system that they were abused.

The recent popular book by feminist writer Susan Faludi, *Backlash – The Undeclared War Against American*

*Women,* is four hundred and sixty pages detailing the injustices Western women continue to endure. She confirms that the Western woman is not yet liberated. She clearly pinpoints major areas which undoubtedly support her statement: marriage, divorce, employment, and the public sector. Yet with all this, no definitive solutions are offered. One begins to feel there are no solutions and that women are at the mercy of the system. Instead of addressing the issues, she more efficiently ignores them and promotes her agenda, which is completely void of the higher calling human beings have. She certainly does not mention anything about making specific changes in the marriage institution. So without a viable marriage system being promoted, it can only be guessed that she approves of a society akin to the one she is living in where there is sexual freedom, unlimited abortions, and illegitimate children. Throughout Ms. Faludi's lengthy book there is an affirmation of injustices in female lives. However, the author is clueless as to the solution because her opinions are devoid of what constitutes authentic liberation – religion.

The very women who claim to be fighting for women's liberation are the very ones who are helping the manmade system further its strategy. Feminists will fight for the right to unlimited abortion and will applaud women entering the Citadel, but will they fight for women to be legally protected within a solid, fair family system that protects their assets and their desire to be stay-at-home moms? The option feminists offer in exchange for marriage and family is independence. Who wants to be totally independent? We are social beings and need one another. These ideas and way of thinking are an escape from finding a better way. Independence in and of itself will not emotionally fulfill human kind. Independence and autonomy is not the answer. They address only the material needs of men and women, and therefore spiritual needs remain unfulfilled.

According to feminists, the liberation of women is closely connected to the actualization of being sexually liberated. Faludi says in her book regarding abortion rights and birth control, "The real change was women's new ability to regulate their fertility without danger or fear – a new freedom that in turn had contributed to dramatic changes, not in the abortion rate, but in female sexual behavior and attitudes... Women were at last at liberty to have sex, like men, on their own terms."[16] Is Faludi referring to legally married women? It is doubtful because she goes on to include stunning statistics that show women's approval of liberal sexual attitudes regarding premarital and extramarital affairs thanks to the birth control pill. Is this why we should be thankful for the various forms of birth control made available to women throughout the world? Through this perspective it seems that for some women the enemy is not the system nor the way it is constructed nor the void of religion in society that is creating all the problems, instead, it is men! The battle seems to be in promoting anything that will bring women exactly where men are in order for women to "mirror" men's behavior.

Women should be focusing on what fulfills them as women instead of copying what men have or what men are doing. Are not women who try to do as men do abandoning their own identity? What makes them so certain that what men have is so great? Why do so many Western women want to opt out of their own sex? Apparently, many feminists have been angry for a long time with men who have, for unknown reasons, been let off the hook regarding their promiscuous behavior. In the West men are not ostracized to the degree women are in regards to their promiscuity. Young men revel among their peers about their illicit affairs and say they have "scored," while women who have "scored" are labeled "loose." This is quite a double

---

[16]*Backlash – The Undeclared War Against the American Women*, p. 403.

standard; however, this is no reason for women to try to "mirror" men. So, many feminists are celebrating because women can control their bodies by subduing fertility and have premarital and extramarital affairs. Just because women can behave as immorally and irresponsibly as men do, is this cause for jubilation? Does the battlefield between men and women come down to who can be sexually freer or more promiscuous? Is the battle between the sexes simply a physical act having nothing to do with moral choices?

Since modern Western civilization has no identifying religion from which to draw its morality from, the public listens instead for cues concerning what is "in," trendy or socially acceptable. Naturally, with such a changing source of guidance, people only become more confused as they try to follow their ever-changing chameleon-like gods. People take refuge in books like Norman Vincent Peal's *The Power of Positive Thinking* or Dale Carnegie's methods of survival in *I'm Okay, You're Okay*. The sources of pop-culture emanate from bits and pieces of what the media dictates and promotes. The voices coming out of political circles and the endless variety of activists also add to pop-culture trends.

# Women and the Work Force

Eileen Boris' exhaustive research in her book *Home to Work* accounts the "homework" industry of the United States from the eighteen hundreds to the current day. American women have played a major role in the development of their country, but they have never been fully recognized. She has not been limited to one or two roles but has always had to take on many more in order to feel worthy.

America in the 1850s found women working as laborers for the East coast cigar industries. These women resided in what were called tenements, where they not only worked but ate, slept, cooked, and cared for their children simultaneously.[17] "Homework," as it was referred to, allowed married women to enhance their lifestyle by adding to the family budget while caring for their children. The notion that women first entered the work force during the 1960s is therefore false. The American woman has played a vital part in the progress of family economic stability and has contributed to society.

By the early 1900s the questions and confusion surrounding the term "feminism" gave rise to suspicions that even within the Women's Movement divisions existed as to what women wanted and needed. In the beginning the word feminism was a term used by women who wanted financial independence, sexual, and political rights.[18] Before the word feminism became dispersed and confused, a feminist wanted to "assert women's individuality over any common womanhood." In other words, real feminism is a term for women who want equal treatment as men under the law in these specific areas. However, by the 1920s, the National Women's Party under Alice Paul "accepted a formalist

---

[17]*Home to Work*, p. 21.
[18]Ibid., p. 158.

jurisprudence that would deny special legal protection for women as a group. Equality under the ERA [Equal Rights Amendment] would negate the women's labor laws because they provided women with 'special' rather than 'legal' treatment." Now women faced the setback and repercussions of having equal legislation without any financial or social equality which led the members of the Women's Bureau to reject and no longer identify themselves with the term feminist.[19]

A greater division now occurred within the Women's Movement. Before the split the Women's Bureau "spoke the language of feminism."[20] It supported women who needed or wanted to work for fair wages and retaliated against women in the society who felt a woman's role in the home as wife and mother was important and necessary, although the American economy by this time was experiencing a depression after the war. The Women's Bureau addressed the very real need at that time for women to help support their families through monetary means. And it rejected any idea that women were the homemakers while men were the breadwinners.[21] According to Boris' research, the Women's Bureau was a unique feminism because it "valued housework, mothering, and self-sacrifice, while it campaigned for equal pay, condemned double sexual as well as economic standards, and fought against occupational segmentation by sex."[22] During this economically unsound time and from the perspective of the Women's Bureau, it would be impossible to request women's role be secured on the homefront as mother when her addition to the family economy was so badly needed. From this it can be safely said that the unstable economy of the United States has for a

---

[19]Ibid., p. 158.
[20]Ibid., p. 158.
[21]Ibid., p. 159.
[22]Ibid., p. 159.

long time forced women to compromise themselves far more than the men in society. While the economy demanded women's roles to adapt and broaden, the males of the society and the political arena kept their status unchanged. Women did not stop having children in order to make things easier for themselves, and this is a significant sign – women instinctively want children and a family life. The Women's Bureau wanted the state to get involved, and with the Children's Bureau's support, it called for state intervention to end the circumstances that pushed families to homework. They concluded that poverty encouraged homework...[23]

Sentiment and legal legislation about homework varied from state to state. In 1923, section II of California's Manufacturing Order prohibited "any women from doing homework after factory hours."[24] This type of law seemed difficult to enforce since the public would probably not agree to the scrutiny and invasion of privacy in their homes in order to regulate such work. By the 1940s women continued to be a part of the work force. They worked in what was termed "cottage factories." This was again work done within a woman's home. Some examples of cottage factories were sewing and typing. The problems with this type of work, at least from the government's perspective, was how it would be controlled, regulated and taxed. Some groups claimed that this type of homework was an unfair burden to the family, especially for children who were said to be raised in unhygienic environments, were often neglected, or who were used as additional labor for the mother. Later, their real concern surfaced. It proved to have little to do with concern for the family unit or the children. They were simply more interested in regulating and making sure that the workers paid their taxes. As time went by the judicial legislation ordered in the 1950s and 60s that "persons who address

---

[23]Ibid., pp. 159-160.
[24]Ibid., p. 163.

envelopes and labels in their homes were employees under the Fair Labor Standards Act."[25]

Clerical home workers were usually married women because it was work that was usually low paying and did not offer health or medical benefits.[26] Although this work often involved more hours than regular jobs, was low paying, and did not offer promotion, women sacrificed themselves in order to stay at home with their small children. Most mothers felt this was not only their responsibility but enjoyed the close contact with their children. Although women chose freely to do this work, there were still political proponents who classified this type of work as exploiting, due to its meager wages. However, many home workers as well as popular media claimed that home-based labor was a way to solve women's conflicting demands between family and career. Nonetheless, studies kept cropping up telling women who were mothers that homework was no substitute for child care. As a result, mothers began to feel more threatened, frustrated and victimized by the system even though they were working long days and giving more than a fair financial contribution to the family.

By 1987 most American women determined for various reasons that to only be a wife or mother was not enough. As one American woman described it: "We're expected to take care of the family, run the house, and hold a job. I accepted low paying, boring work with no opportunities for advancement and no benefits because I get to stay home with my daughter." One researcher determined that such women and attitudes reflect the need women have to "feel productive."[27]

---

[25]Ibid., p. 305.
[26]Ibid., p. 306.
[27]Ibid., pp. 331-334.

## Out of the Home and into the Work Force

"*I am woman, hear me roar, in numbers too big to ignore, and I know too much to go back and pretend. But I'm still an embryo, with a long, long way to go, until I make my brother understand...*"[28]

Such lyrics vocalized the strongly felt sentiments the vast majority of American women were identifying with by the 1970s. Although the American woman had proven to be a hard-working member of society, she did not feel she was regarded as equal to men. As the song suggests, the Women's Movement had come full term, and women were finished with their long embryonic sleep in the womb. They were now mature and smart enough to venture outside their sheltered, oppressive state. But there were many mountains to climb, and changes were slow in coming. In fact, some believed the movement had great potential but believed the leaders lost their way and drastically failed in terms of what women really needed. Indeed, a battle between the sexes was underway. The enlightenment of the Western woman finally occurred after a long incubation period of confinement and frustration. The woman had never been treated with equal respect or rights. She had been treated inhumanely, irrespective of her donations towards progress and her undying support and sacrifice to family. For centuries the American woman had no legal right to own property, run a business or have her own economic status. As recently as 1988, some American states still enforced laws which kept wives subservient to their husbands. Under these laws a wife was not allowed economic independence, so to open a checking account or buy or sell property, she had to obtain her husband's permission and signature. The right to vote was also slow in coming. Women have only been filling out voting forms for the past 75 years.

---

[28] Popular song sung by Helen Reddy.

According to Susan Faludi's book, 80% of females are still stuck in dead-end jobs that are almost always relegated to females, i.e., clerks, secretaries, receptionists or sales positions, and nearly 75% of full-time employed women were earning under $20,000 annually.[29] Additionally, during the Reagan administration, statistics showed there were two million single mothers who were claiming to be head of households and close to five million women under the poverty level.[30] Today, more American women and mothers are working outside the home for various reasons. According to a news article in 1993 projecting government figures, the number of mothers who work is a growing trend. In 1992, 67.2% of women with children under the age of eighteen were employed either in full- or part-time jobs. This percentage was up from 47.4% in 1975 and 58.9% in 1983. A majority of mothers with preschool age children stayed home or only worked part time. 31% of women with a newborn and 18% with two or more children are employed full time.[31] In another report entitled, "Government Finds U.S. Working Women Stressed, Underpaid," working women's sentiments regarding their jobs were detailed. Many women complained of having to do better than the men they worked with. "You have to be better than any males in your job. You have to juggle family and work and still do better just to prove you are a career person and a mother," stated one woman.[32] Karen Nussbaum, director of the Labor Department's Women's Bureau, said that a survey launched by President Clinton's administration discovered how working women felt about their jobs and that it "unveiled the anger" most American women have regarding their status. Besides being overworked and overstressed,

---

[29]*Backlash – The Undeclared War Against the American Women*, p. xiii.
[30]Ibid., p. xvii.
[31]Ana Suarez-Veciana, "More Women Sacrifice to Stay Home with Kids," *Knight Ridder Tribune, Arizona Republic,* Sept. 5, 1993.
[32]Labor Department Women's Bureau findings, *Arab News,* Oct. 16, 1994.

women were still not earning the same amount for the same job men performed. "The Labor Department said women typically earn .71 cents for every dollar earned by a man. The problem is worse for women from racial and ethnic minority groups." Nussbaum said she "didn't expect to hear much about discrimination but respondents brought it up repeatedly."[33] And finally, statistics from the Children's Defense Fund reported that more than 15 million children in the United States in 1994 were living in poverty.[34] It can be safely assumed that most of these children come from households with single parents, most likely women. This further confirms that American women are still living under much oppression and face numerous injustices largely due to their unequal earning power in comparison with men.

Professor Marianne Moody Jennings, who teaches legal and ethical studies at Arizona State University, says that NOW (National Organization for Women) is headed by the elite women in society who are wealthy, educated and cared for, and "they are also absolutely clueless about women, their needs and their challenges. They claim the imprimatur of all women. Their world is expensive, cold, unrealistic and isolated." Professor Jennings asks them, "What of the secretaries, receptionists, waitresses and factory line workers? They struggle domestically, economically and physically to carve out a life... and hope that the transmissions on their Ford Escorts hold up... Their wages and status remain low." And she adds, "What of the women who are at home with their children... all in exchange for this description: 'She's just a housewife.' For purposes of the Women's Movement, they are non-existent." And she rightfully speaks for women who did as they were told – they got their education and are now working professionals. "These are the women who were told to become accountants,

---

[33] Ibid.
[34] "Child Poverty Worse in 30 Years," *Arab News,* Oct. 8, 1994, p. 8.

lawyers, and managers so that their lives would be better. They went to school, got their degrees, married and had children. You can spot them easily by the dark circles under their eyes. The great purple-eyed female genius. NOW is not for them. Who has the time?"[35]

## How the System Stigmatizes the Mother

Although a poor economy forces many mothers to work, it seems that others in the West are leaving home to get away from the stigma attached to being "just a mother." Sadly, when a woman in America stays home to raise children, she is not allowed the peace and security of knowing that the system upholds and recognizes her role as wife or mother. She is promised nothing if she should find herself facing divorce. Therefore, a woman who does not work may feel insecure and anxious because as attorney Frances Leonard says, "Place your hopes and dreams in the long future of your marriage; but recognize that the state won't back you in the gamble. When you forego your own career opportunities in the expectation of joint future returns, you place yourself at serious risk; and no amount of bitterness and recrimination will finance you if things don't work out in the end." In Ms. Leonard's book, *Women and Money*, she confirms that most women who go through divorce do not come away from the process like the old stories we used to hear about – the "rich divorcées."[36] In 1990, only 15.5% of divorced women were legally awarded alimony payments. And astonishingly, a mere 32.3% of divorced women who asked for a part of the property settlement got any.[37] In 1980 in New York State, the expense for legal representation for a disputed divorce case

---

[35]"Which Class of Women Counts for NOW?" *Arizona Republic*, July 24, 1994.
[36]*Women Pay More*, p. 119.
[37]Ibid., p. 120.

was six thousand dollars. Today, attorney's fees can reach a whopping $50,000.[38] Jennifer Gordon, head of the San Francisco Bar Association's Family Law Division, says, "If you're making $40,000, $50,000 even $60,000 a year, I don't see how you can afford a family lawyer at $200.00 an hour."[39] Here is another American institution reserved for society's elite. And Western marriage laws guarantee the woman nothing. A successful settlement may be by chance or depend upon if she can afford good legal council.

By taking a closer look at how much money working mothers earn, the real picture is becoming more dismal. Firstly, most women are still in traditional jobs. For the sake of argument, take the scenario of a married woman who has one child under school age. Without deducting expenses for food, rent, phone and electric (assuming the husband is paying for these), her entry level secretarial job pays $18,000 annually. The first automatic deduction is the large portion for taxes. Car payments on an average run $200 per month. Daycare expenses total at least $80 per week. Gas, car maintenance and insurance must be included as well. To start a modest wardrobe for a working woman will not come cheap either, and these are just the necessary expenses. After all that, what will she have left over for emergencies, vacations or perhaps a little luxury?

Under most circumstances working wives are contributing towards the rent, utilities, and other household expenses. With this in mind, the picture is bleaker for a woman's financial gain in terms of personal economic stability. It is doubtful that such earning potential really heightens a woman's self-esteem or level of financial security. Certainly, such little income cannot be considered as paving the way towards financial independence.

---

[38]Ibid., p. 122.
[39]Ibid., p. 123.

Additionally, if mothers are leaving their children in daycare centers to work at low-paying jobs which do not necessarily give them enough in return, then this must further humiliate and frustrate her as a woman, wife and mother. It is very likely that the stigma placed on mothers who stay home is greater than most imagine. Maybe women are leaving their homes in hopes of rebuilding their self-worth, even if it means settling for a low-paying, substandard job.

## The Force That Is Negligent

At this point one may rightfully ask, "Where are all the loud, opinionated feminists, and what are they really doing to help women in these vital areas that need reworking?" In all fairness, the label "feminist" does not suit them. The word feminist is akin to feminine, womanly, lady-like, gentle and nurturing. But feminism and its rhetoric and philosophies have nothing to do with any of these admirable traits. Instead, these women encourage the manmade system by their silence. As it is now Western-style marriage does not require a man to be responsible. Imagine the tables turned on men, obligating or legislating them responsible. What would happen? Maybe there would be a significant decline in marriages because the system lacks the religious and moral basis through which to enforce such responsibility.

In 1985, only 50% of 8.8 million female head of households with children after divorce were receiving child support from the fathers. And only 50% of these got the full amount legally awarded to them by the judge.[40] In 1988, the Federal Office of Child Support Enforcement located only 5 billion of the 25 billion "dead beat" dads who were delinquent in paying what the judges had ordered them to pay.[41] With these kinds of statistics most would conclude

---

[40]*Backlash – The Undeclared War Against the American Women*, p. 24.
[41]Ibid., p. 24.

that there is a need for laws to be implemented and enforced to oblige fathers to pay child support.

Most child support that is awarded is grossly under what the real costs of raising a child amounts to. Author Faludi does not see going after fathers as the viable solution. Instead, she recommends what the Federal Advisory Council concluded in 1982: "The most effective way to correct the post-divorce inequities between the sexes is simple: correct pay inequality in the work force. If the wage gap were wiped out between the sexes... one half of the female-headed households would be instantly lifted out of poverty."[42] Okay, so what about the other half? And in what way is this going to make men more responsible towards their children? Why are feminists negotiating such raw deals on behalf of women? Do women want to have children without fathers? Has anyone stopped this merry-go-round to reflect that perhaps the children of the future might one day want to know who their fathers are? The quest for autonomy in these terms is too self-serving. These issues are being ignored, which is proof that the system is not pro-family or pro-woman.

## **Birth of the Super Woman — Necessity, Not Choice**

Due to this unfair system, women are expected to become "super women." They must do it all or lose it all. If they choose to get married, they must be mother, wife and career person simultaneously. Being a wife and mother is definitely not considered enough. Some women are super moms for a period of years, but eventually this burden takes its toll, especially if they do not have the earning potential to make it all worth the effort. At first, burnout comes in subtle ways. It might be experienced as simple fatigue, slight depression or insomnia. They work hard and need an

---

[42]Ibid., p. 25.

escape. Some join the men at happy hour, and some end up consulting physicians wondering why they feel the way they do. They may start drinking or get addicted to prescription tranquilizers or anti-depressants. What these women may not realize is that their physical and emotional problems stem directly from their specific place in life as a woman.

Most assuredly, the reason women are not making great strides has nothing to do with their lack of ability or intelligence. Women are smart and extremely capable. So why are they not getting ahead? Clearly, the two main reasons point to the woman having the roles of wife and mother. Mothers deal and solve numerous problems and issues that fathers simply do not. By performing the necessary time-consuming jobs of laundry, shopping, cooking and cleaning, the wife frees her husband to work the overtime, thereby making him the breadwinner. He becomes indispensable to his company. He is promoted and then comes home to a quiet, orderly home environment. His laundry is done, his shirts are pressed, and his dinner is waiting at the table. According to Western practice, one may form the opinion that motherhood and being married is not necessarily a plus in terms of a woman's happiness or success in life.

So can career-oriented women have happier, easier lives? In Terri Apter's comprehensive study of successful women, she says, "They [successful career women] did not believe that they could have it all: they believed that they could have what they wanted by giving up what other women had. They were modern in deliberately counting the cost of marriage which women are far more likely to do today..."[43] Thus, the practice is confirmed that to really succeed in American society, women must do as men do in their education and careers. In order to continue their quest

---

[43] *Working Women Don't Have Wives – Professional Success in the 1990s*, p. 206.

set into motion by the Women's Movement, they urgently feel the need to continue changing their roles as wife and mother.

All mothers can agree that having small children to care for is exhausting, but fathers rarely feel this way because they are not the primary caregivers. Women not only experience depression more than men, but as mothers they suffer more fatigue and mental and/or emotional difficulties. Even with a father's help, the woman is still prone to be more emotionally and physically drained. While it may have something to do with the way mothers feel more strongly attached to their children, it is more likely because many working mothers still do all the household chores.

Apter's found that women who were financially successful were typically single or at least childless. Women who never married explained that they saw marriage at odds with their career commitments. Those who were divorced or separated said that their career commitment had been an important factor in the breakdown of the marriage. In addition to this, Apter concludes, "For these women the task was to keep guard on themselves and to change, to learn in more and more detail how to think like men: that was their path to success."[44]

It becomes clearer that in order for the modern woman to have much chance of becoming financially secure, she must hold off on family life. Additionally, she must plan on keeping this career throughout most of her life in order to get ahead. The well-known suffragist, Susan B. Anthony, is a testament to this fact. She never married and remained childless all her life.

The women's liberation rhetoric tells women over and over again that in order to be successful and happy people, they must put themselves first and their children and families

---

[44]Ibid., p. 206.

thereafter. They must value themselves in much the same way as men do in regards their job. "Their [women's] willingness to do this may be symptomatic of the new work culture: the idea that we are what our job is, that the value of our job is what we earn along with the perks that rail in the wake of a high salary. Have women not fallen prey to the feminist mystique, whereby they put careers first and either forgo family life or treat it as an aside? Has women's liberation not led to the devaluation of women's traditional input into future generations and into the community and into the home?"[45]

## Gender Discrimination

Gender discrimination is yet another form of assault against women. In the workplace women face sex discrimination the moment they apply for the same job that a man does. Although it is wrong (even illegal in America), it is still easily practiced. Female job applicants are often asked personal and scrutinizing questions about whether or not they are planning on having children. Companies are concerned about maternity leave and try to avoid the financial loss connected to it. Odds are a man will be hired instead. This type of gender discrimination is common and difficult, if not impossible, to prove. Men are also often times hired over women because men are usually more free to work overtime or relocate.

In *Women Pay More* startling findings add fuel to the fire when women realize how often they face sex discrimination in America. Everything from haircuts, dry cleaning, clothing costs to car repairs and purchases are areas where women pay more than men simply because they are female.[46] Here is an example: A young woman was looking

---

[45]Ibid., p. 211.
[46]*Women Pay More (and How to Put a Stop to It)*, p. xi.

through a rack of ski jackets in the men's department. The store clerk approached her and said, "Your jackets are over there." The woman responded, "Over there costs thirty dollars more."[47] Another example is that women pay more for medical services in comparison to men. She not only makes more doctor visits, but a woman who sees a doctor for the same illness a man does is often given more tests and more medications. On top of that a woman is often requested to return for a follow-up visit, while this request is seldom given to a male patient. The American Medical Association says the reasons for this "are not clear."[48] And still more astonishingly common is the fact that women pay more when they purchase automobiles. In 1990, an investigation in Chicago sought to discover if salespeople discriminate against people. Posing as car buyers, the research group went to 165 automobile dealerships acting as if they wanted to buy a new car. The investigation was controlled to "factor out people's bargaining abilities" by giving all of the posing buyers the same exact mode of action. They were all clothed professionally and said the exact same things to the salespeople. In addition, they all used identical body language. The findings were as follows: white women paid 40% higher markups in comparison to white men, African American males paid two times what white men paid, and African American women paid three times more than white men.[49]

---

[47]Ibid., p. 12.
[48]Ibid., p. 28.
[49]Ibid., p. 7.

# The Media

## The Mighty Media

For a vast majority of people living in the West, the media has taken the place of real education. In fact, many people think the media is educational, and they are quick to believe everything it tells them because they are convinced journalists have integrity. They are told that the media is a responsible enterprise. Many people worldwide rely heavily upon the media as their main source of information and knowledge.

The media is a politically run and motivated entity. As such, it should be carefully interpreted only in this mind frame, and it certainly should not be considered a substitute for real education. Ben A. Bagdikian has firsthand knowledge about the depth of power possessed by the media. A Pulitzer prize-winning journalist and former dean of the Graduate School of Journalism at the University of California in Berkeley states, "Americans, like most people, get images of the world from their newspapers, magazines, radio, television, books and movies."[50] The media has the power to change and manipulate the inner beliefs, moral convictions, and personal opinions of the public at large. What is especially important for the public to recognize is that the media is no different than any other corporation or business, and, as such, it has economic interests at the forefront. Bagdikian continues, "Authorities have always recognized that to control the public, they must control information. The initial possessor of news and ideas has political power – the power to disclose or conceal, to announce some parts and not others, to hold back until opportunistic moments, to predetermine the interpretation of

---

[50] *The Media Monopoly*, p. xxvi.

what is revealed."⁵¹ Therefore, people who listen to the media as a viable information resource gather information slowly and sporadically and do so with the risk of receiving only fragmented parts, which may not make sense even if what is projected is true. And worse, it very often leaves one without any true convictions and with a lot of rhetoric that can possibly be false.

The most alarming revelation Bagdikian divulged is that the ownership of the big media companies is now controlled and managed by a small, elite group. Where once fifty national and multinational corporations ran the majority of media production, by 1983 it had been whittled down to only twenty. Although there are hundreds and thousands of smaller firms in action, the impact of these less powerful firms is nearly non-existent. For example, even though there are 3,000 publishers in the United States, only five of them generate the majority of income.[52] In 1983, there were only eleven corporations who managed the majority of national media. The number used to be twenty.[53] In periodical circulation the yearly income goes to two firms, whereas it used to go to twenty. And in book publishing, what used to go to eleven now goes to only five. As for television and the movie makers, their status remains unchanged with three television networks and four movie production studios.[54] Bagdikian also said, "The United States has an impressive array of mass communications. There are 1,700 daily newspapers, 11,000 magazines, 9,000 radio and 1,000 television stations, 2,500 book publishers, and 7 movie studios." He explains that if every one of these had different owners, then there might be around 25,000 individual corporations able to represent a wide variety of media

---

[51]Ibid., p. xxvi.
[52]Ibid., p. ix.
[53]Ibid., p. ix.
[54]Ibid., p. x.

projection. But he confirms that this is not the case. Only fifty corporations represent the American media.[55]

Based on these statistics it is possible that the Western public, if they remain naïve to the media, could be slowly and rhythmically brainwashed. It is known that the media has conveniently told partial truths and has the power to manipulate news. It certainly can direct attention away from important issues to what it prefers to project.[56] It can also draw our attention away from something perhaps more important only to fill it with something trivial. Worse, it can omit altogether whatever is of greater importance. An example of the media's self-interest was seen back in 1966 when Fred Friendly felt he had a moral obligation to resign as Acting President of CBS News because the network would not allow the report of a vitally important Senate hearing about the Vietnam War. Instead, the authorities told Friendly that he and his team should run a fifth daytime rerun of the *I Love Lucy* show. They warned him that one delayed episode of the "Lucy" show would not be approved by shareholders. They were convinced that to delay such a popular show would create a great financial loss. The company's stockholders would be clearly upset, and that was all that had to be said.[57]

This shows the media's mentality and how it makes decisions about what takes priority and what does not. It is time the media and its few directive leading corporations, its leaders, and shareholders come under the American public's scrutiny. Naturally, when an information source is being biased or led by the economy and favored politics of the time, then it is definitely time to stop relying upon it as a viable source of education.

---

[55]Ibid., p. xxviii.
[56]Ibid., p. xxviii.
[57]Ibid., p. xxix.

## Media Portrayal of the Islamic World

The media has for years portrayed Muslims, Islam and Arabs in a negative light. As a unified nation (brotherhood), Muslims are not willing to sit back without standing up to defend themselves, especially when their religion, way of life, and legal laws are continually being criticized and attacked.

Contrary to what the media projects, Islam is a religion of peace, not war. It is a religion of justice, not injustice. Islam is a religion of unity, not factions. And Muslims have always been more tolerant of other religious groups than the latter have been toward them. What is apparent is that whatever the media says is quite literally and unquestionably believed.

On the local news in Jeddah, Saudi Arabia, actual filmed out-takes were aired of Israeli soldiers viciously beating a Muslim woman who was only trying to protect her unarmed son. The vision was one of abusive authority, human cruelty, and unfair force used against a defenseless, unarmed woman. From any just person's perspective these soldiers were overstepping their authority. The woman's son was a Palestinian youth who, at most, was throwing stones at Israeli soldiers. Does Western media project the truth about such Palestinian and Israeli clashes? No! Western news channels project a completely different angle and rewrite a whole new version with the Israeli soldiers as victims. Western viewers will not see an Israeli soldier beating up a woman or using unusual brute force. All one sees in the Western media is the Israeli soldiers apparently defending themselves with guns – against stones!

The Western public should begin to ask more questions. For example, why have some Palestinians martyred themselves if they do not feel their cause is worthy? Why does the Western media enlarge upon the image of the "fanatical" Palestinian youths who, by their stone throwing, incite war and strife? In reality, they are only attempting to defend themselves against an entity encroaching upon rights to their religion, land and life. Precious few Westerners will be allowed to know the truth about Palestine until it is possibly too late.

## Western Scholars and Islam

The problem of negatively portraying Arabs, Islam and Muslims is not a new phenomenon. Fred Halliday, a leading British author and philosopher, specializes in Arab/Islamic studies. His research includes the politics and history of the Arab world, and he is a professor of international relations at the London School of Economics and Political Science. According to an interview with Mr. Halliday, he said there is a "widespread hostility to Muslims."[58] This is due to issues of race, color and immigration. He also intimated that the Islamic revolution in Iran helped to increase hostilities and created an enflamed prejudice about Islam from both Europe and the United States. He said, "The Iranians who held the American diplomats hostage – that more than anything else – fixed with their mentality of Hollywood the stereotype of the aggressive Muslim." This shows that Hollywood was further fueled to establish within the public's psyche the cruel, abusive Arab who oppresses, especially women. Halliday also directs one's attention to the widely televised broadcasts about sieges of Muslims worldwide. Battlefields in Bosnia, Palestine, Kashmir and Chechnya are places of great unrest and not only representative of "Muslim problems" but "human problems." In these areas where threats, war and death constantly bombard Muslims, it leaves them powerless to project Islam in its true light. An additional setback for these war-torn areas is a lack of adequate support from Muslim countries enjoying peace and prosperity.

---

[58]Fred Halliday, "Islam in the West: The Causes of Prejudice," interview by Abdullah Homouda, *Arab News,* June 22, 1995, p. 11.

The only real hope in strengthening relations between the East and West is by education and a willingness to be open-minded. Dr. Carl Brown, former director of the Interdisciplinary Program in Near Eastern Studies at Princeton University, specializes in history of the Near East and North Africa with an emphasis on the Arab-speaking world. During an interview with journalist Afshin Molavi, Dr. Brown said that "a lot of Americans are not really all that aware of the Middle East, and a lot of Arabs are not all that aware of America. This reinforces our belief that the education system as well as the media are not fulfilling their duty to spread a true picture of Islam in the eyes of the Westerners." However, Brown asserts that Thomas Friedman, a New York Times correspondent and author of *From Beirut to Jerusalem,* "himself says that he grew up as a Jew in a very orthodox Jewish family with all of the stereotypes about how great Israel was and how bad the Arabs were and in his book moves away from this with a very human notion of the way the two sides don't understand each other."[59] Through this exchange one can better understand Islam, the West, and the need for a firm grounding for future relations. There must be a way to put a final end to the perpetuation of prejudice and misinterpretation about Islam.

Francis Lamand, a French doctor of law, professor, diplomat, international lawyer and president of the French association Islam and the West, found the "realities of the Islamic world" while in Kuwait in 1970 when serving as a diplomat. While there he was also a professor of the Shariah Faculty at the University of Kuwait. Soon after, Lamand became a "militant," as he describes himself in an interview with journalist Lamis Moufti. He said that after realizing

---

[59]Dr. Carl Brown, "Bringing the West and Islamic World Closer: Let's Begin the Process with Educated People," interview by Afshin Molavi, *Arab News,* January 24, 1994, p. 13.

Islam's realities, it drove deep into him a great desire to help foster good relations between Islamic and Western cultures. "Islam has a lot to teach the West," he added. The second religion in France, Islam's community is comprised of 4 million people.

Lamand stressed that for good relations to be promoted, there must somehow come about an acceptance of Islam in both Europe and the United States, especially since it is a growing religion in both regions. There is a need to foster understanding and integrate certain norms and values which, he claimed, "have a de facto existence with the French law." To Lamand and others "this is incumbent upon governments not only in France but in all Western states."[60]

In his interview with *Arab News,* Dr. Caesar Farah, Chairman of South Asian and Middle Eastern Studies at the University of Minnesota, felt "there was considerable interest in Islam in America. Unfortunately, it does not always result from any educated and scientific awareness," he added. In other words, he affirmed the desire for knowledge but acknowledged the lack of resources. This discussion disclosed that Americans are by and large "apolitical" and "their opinions tend to be shaped from what they see, read or hear without the opportunity to analyze or criticize." In his opinion talking about Islam as a "good religion" is "more tolerant than others have been toward it... We cannot rely on the press to project it properly."[61]

### Prince Charles at the Oxford Centre for Islamic Studies

In October of 1993, Prince Charles addressed the Oxford Centre for Islamic Studies. A major patron of the Centre, he was asked to speak about his knowledge of Islam.

---

[60]Frances Lamand, "Cultural Open-Mindedness a Must," interview by Moufti Lamis, *Arab News,* January 24, 1994, p. 13.

[61]Dr. Caesar Farah, "Move to Set Up Islamic Research Center in U.S.," interview by Habib Shaikh, *Arab News,* April 16, 1993.

The following paragraphs are excerpts from his speech:

"The depressing fact is, that despite the advances in technology and mass communications of the second half of the 20th century, despite mass travel, the intermingling of the races, the ever-growing reduction – or so we believe – about the mysteries of our world, misunderstandings between Islam and the West continue... As far as the West is concerned, this cannot be because of ignorance. There are one billion Muslims worldwide. Many millions live in Commonwealth. Ten million of them live in the West and around one million live in Britain. Our own Islamic community has been growing and flourishing for decades... It is odd, in many ways, that misunderstandings between Islam and the West should persist. For that which binds our two worlds together is so much more powerful than that which divides us. We share many key values in common... Another obvious Western prejudice is to judge the position of women in Islamic society by the extreme cases. The rights of Muslim women to property and inheritance, to some protection if divorced, and to the conducting of business were rights prescribed by the Qur'an 1400 years ago. In Britain, at least, some of these were novel even to my grandmother's generation!"

He goes on to remind the West of its apparent forgetfulness and indebtedness to the Muslim world, stating, "We have underestimated the importance of 800 years of Islamic society and culture in Spain between the 8th and 15th centuries... to the preservation of classical learning during the Dark Ages, and to the first flowerings of the Renaissance... Not only did Muslim Spain gather and preserve the intellectual content of ancient Greek and Roman civilization, it also interpreted and expanded upon that civilization and made a vital contribution of its own in so many fields... in science, astronomy, mathematics, algebra... law, history, medicine, pharmacology, optics, agriculture, architecture, theology and music... Many of the traits on which modern Europe prides itself came to it from Muslim Spain. Diplomacy, free trade, open borders, the techniques of academic research, of anthropology, etiquette, fashion, alternative medicine, hospitals, all came from this great city of cities. Medieval Islam was a religion of remarkable tolerance for its time, allowing Jews and Christians the right to practice their inherited beliefs and setting an example which was not, unfortunately, copied for many centuries in the West..."

Near the end of Prince Charles' speech, he said, "More than this, Islam can teach us today a way of understanding and living in a world which Christianity itself is poorer for having lost. At the heart of Islam is its preservation of an integral view of the universe. Islam refuses to separate man and nature, religion and science, mind and matter, and has preserved a metaphysical and unified view of ourselves and the world around us... But the West gradually lost this integrated vision of the world with Copernicus and Descartes and the coming of the scientific revolution."[62]

What a beautiful representation of some of the facts about Islam, its history and Arab contributions to the world. But how many Westerners have heard this speech in total? How many fearful minds and hearts could have been comforted and enlightened by this message? Did the Western media advertise this advocacy for true Islamic understanding? No, because the media's agenda is at odds with what Islam stands for.

Although strides have been made for Islamic awareness, such as the public speech of Prince Charles, it might be of interest to also realize that through the untiring efforts of many Muslim activists based in the West, educational facilities and institutes are growing to further

---

[62]Prince Charles, "Islam and the West," *Arab News,* October 27, 1993.

propagate Islamic knowledge. It is commonly agreed that authentic information on Islam is a much neglected area in the Western education curriculum. However, there is a growing awareness due to the efforts of Islamic foundations and centers on many American college campuses.

The construction of a major Islamic institute is currently under development in Edmonton, Canada. It will teach children from kindergarten to grade 12. The institute will be a government based, full-time operation. It is expected to accommodate as many as 650 students. Edmonton has a large Muslim community of 20,000, and growing. It also has four mosques.[63]

A new Islamic center in Rome, Italy has recently opened. This center took nearly eleven years to complete and is located adjacent to the River Tiber near the Vatican. The minaret of the mosque is forty feet high, and the building is comprised of 30,000 square meters. It has an educational facility, a library, and halls used for various gatherings. It is beautifully decorated with ceramic Moroccan-styled tiles. There are nearly one million Muslims in Italy, and approximately 85,000 Muslims live in Rome.[64]

In addition to these Islamic educational facilities, there are many mosques throughout America. In the city of Los Angeles alone there are forty mosques. Information about Islam can be easily obtained through contact with a mosque because they usually have libraries or will know where to find more reliable resources on Islam. So there is a shimmer of hope for Islam to be fairly represented through the media, but it is a process that is long overdue.

---

[63] Abdul Wahab Bashir, "Islamic Institute in Edmonton," *Arab News*, 1995.
[64] "Rome Opens Islamic Center," *Islamic Horizons*, Indiana: Islamic Society of North America, Sept/Oct, 1995, p. 14.

## The Negative Portrayal and Media Bloopers

In 1992, *Vogue,* the international fashion magazine, ran a two-page advertisement for a woman's perfume, *Bijan.* The costly two-page ad pictured two women, one positioned on each page, as if opposing one another. The woman on the right page was wearing a baseball cap and holding a baseball bat, smiling beautifully. Beneath was the caption, "Women should be bright, wild, flirty, fun, eccentric, tough, bold and very very Bijan." The woman on the left page was wearing a black *tarhah* (head covering) and black *'abayah* (head to foot outer covering), undoubtedly portraying a Muslim woman. Unlike the opposite page there was no American flag, no fair skin, and no smile. This caption read, "Women should be obedient, grateful, modest, respectful, submissive and very very serious."[65]

Bijan is an international cosmetics and fragrance empire and is successfully marketed in Muslim countries. The ad was executed with a high level of precision – it did not necessarily use offensive words to describe the Muslim woman, but the choice to use a Muslim-looking woman instead of any other woman is exploitative from a Muslim's point of view. To insert a Muslim-looking woman into such a magazine is a serious breach of morality from Islam's standpoint. In addition, to intentionally omit the American flag from the Muslim's side is making a blatant nationalistic and racist statement by sending the subliminal message that a Muslim cannot be American or fair-skinned. Finally, the words used to describe both women were not absolute opposites, but they appeared to be so at first glance. The ad's wording obviously favored the American woman and was intended to protect her image. If the words had been exact opposites, they would have sabotaged her character and

---

[65]*Vogue Magazine,* April, 1992.

would have read, "Women should be rebellious, demanding, immodest, disrespectful, intolerant and very very silly."

American Muslims have begun to organize themselves against such negative attacks on Islam. In September, 1994, angered Muslims picketed stores throughout America that stocked a get-well card which used a veiled woman and contained a highly offensive play on words associated with Islam. Due to such efforts, the card was eventually taken off the shelves.

## Gains and Setbacks

The American-Arab Discrimination Committee in Washington has been a solid impetus confronting the elements which misrepresent Islam, Muslims and Arabs. The past president of the ADC wrote to the Disney Studios chairman, Jeffrey Katzenberg, to ask that the lyrics to *Aladdin* be changed prior to the film's video release to the public. The original song went something like, "I come from a land, from a faraway place, where the caravan camels roam. Where they cut off your ear, if they don't like your face, it's barbaric, but hey, it's home."[66] This kind of negative portrayal could very well have planted a lasting image of cruelty and barbarism of the Arab culture into the minds of its young viewers.

The ADC has also successfully halted the closing of a northern Virginia mosque due to zoning laws, as well as stopping the distribution of a United States Marine Corps training film which depicted Muslims as terrorists who were a threat to the West.[67] The ADC also counter-attacked a twelve page article entitled, *Women of the Veil,* which ran June 28th, 1993, in the *Atlanta Journal and Constitution.* Its

---

[66] Dr. Michael Saba, "ADC Wins a Few for American Muslims," *Arab News,* May 18, 1993.
[67] Ibid.

author misinterpreted and portrayed Muslim women as oppressed and Islam as a religion that strips women of their rights. The series of articles included themes such as, *Imprisoned for Love* and *Using Rape to Settle Scores.*[68] The ADC confronted the *Bijan* perfume ad by sending a letter which read, "Being Muslim and American is not a contradiction and therefore should not be portrayed as such..." The letter's intent was to remind Bijan's management that the United States is a multi-cultural society. Bijan should also be aware that there is a growing population of American-Muslim women. The ADC received a written apology from Bijan and was told that the ADC's objections would be taken into account.[69]

In addition, the ADC "successfully prosecuted a discrimination case against now-defunct Pan American World Airways." The ADC accused the airline of subjecting Muslims, Arabs and Arab-Americans to heightened security searches, luggage checks, personal questioning, and in some instances, strip searches. Although Pan Am denied the allegations, they settled the case out of court by "paying a sum to the ADC, the ACLU (American Civil Liberties Union), and one of the victims of its security screenings."[70]

The bombing of the Alfred P. Murrah Federal building in Oklahoma in 1995 is another example of the widely accepted notion, enforced through the media, that terrorism emanates from the Middle East. Immediately following the bombing and before any suspects were named, the national media cited anonymous sources saying witnesses saw Middle-Eastern looking men running from the building seconds before the blast. Within a few hours mosques across the United States began receiving threatening and obscene messages, many recorded on answering machines. Radio

---

[68]Ibid.
[69]Ibid.
[70]Ibid.

talk show hosts fanned the flames and encouraged listeners to call in and vent their anger on the "Muslim baby killers." According to Peter Mansfield, the immediate reaction from both Britain and the United States was to blame the bombing on "Islamic extremism" even before the first suspect was caught. Newspaper headlines screamed, "Muslim Bombers." Not surprisingly, there were no apologies made to Muslims for these slanderous attacks after the arrest of Timothy McVeigh, an American citizen, a Christian and former Marine Corps private. As Mansfield put it, "The event revealed something truly alarming about the United States today."[71]

The Washington-based Council on American-Islamic Relations documented the two and a half days of speculation about the suspicion of Muslims in America following the horrific bombing of the federal building. Muslims experienced physical assault, shootings, rock throwing, arson, threats and verbal abuse due solely to the media's rush to judgement. Gunshots were fired into an Oklahoma mosque on both April 19th and 20th, and a Muslim woman was shot at in Chicago while walking down the street. Another American Muslim woman's home was damaged by rock throwing vandals, and she suffered a miscarriage of her six-month old fetus, allegedly due to her emotional anxiety. Later at the hospital, her husband tried to hide the fact that they were Muslims and that he was Arab out of fear they would not treat his wife properly.

If this is not enough, other incidents included shots being fired into an Indiana mosque, and a Muslim was attacked with a knife in an Oklahoma parking lot. Students in a 7th grade class were told by their teacher that "Muslims bombed Oklahoma city because Allah told them to do so." After class, a Muslim student was beaten by his classmates.

---

[71]Peter Mansfield, "The Questions Raised by Oklahoma," *Arab News*, 1995.

A contractor working for an American-Muslim doctor in McLean, Virginia, told the doctor to "go back to your [expletive] country."[72]

Why is it that public reaction is so violent toward innocent Muslims when another Muslim is at or assumed to be at fault? Is there not a double standard between this and other fringe groups? Take Ireland as an example. Even though Catholics and Protestants are gunning each other down and blowing up innocent bystanders along with each other, there is absolutely no fallout from these terrorist acts in the United States. That is, Protestants and Catholics are not being discriminated against, nor are they living in fear.

Prior to the Oklahoma bombing, it was apparent that a majority of the American public believed that such terrorist acts were perpetrated by outside forces, not American citizens. They had been led into believing that most violent acts come from extremists with exotic, Arab-sounding names.

Professor Wilkinson is one of the world's foremost experts on terrorism. He is a professor of International Relations and heads the Centre for the Study of Terrorism and Political Violence at St. Andrews University in Scotland. Professor Wilkinson had this to say about the N.Y. World Trade Center bombing: "It appears that the World Trade Center group [responsible for the bombing] was put together in the U.S. rather than as the arm of some state."[73] He points out that with a whopping 1.3 million violent crimes in the past decade in the United States and 20,000 homicides – this ordinary "home-based" crime seems to be more a threat from an American's perspective than the threat of "terrorism."[74]

---

[72]Afshin Molavi, "Muslim-Bashing Follows Oklahoma Bombing," *Arab News,* May 24, 1995.
[73]Paula Sands, "World Sees Terrorists as New Enemy," *Arab News,* April 26, 1995, p. 11.
[74]Ibid.

With the United States current stance on gun control and its liberal allowance for citizens to purchase and use guns, the people who blame law enforcement should acknowledge that for the very freedoms they claim as their right, there will always be repercussions. "American laws permit groups to operate with relative ease."[75]

It is undeniable that the media has successfully capitalized on political unrest in the Middle East. By carefully edited film clips, sound bites, and access to always "unidentified" high level sources (to name a few), the media's propaganda campaign has achieved success. The brainwashing of the Western mind against Islam will be a brief victory, however, and devout Muslims know it.

---

[75]Ibid.

# Life Without God

## The Impact of Civilization Without Culture

If civilization is the effect man has on nature by using his knowledge and innate intelligence to create the world around him and culture includes the influence religion has upon man and his nature,[76] then a civilization void of religion, comprised of only manmade laws, would be missing some of the necessary components to legislate a sound, morally viable system for human life as God intended. Such a civilization could be labeled as *jahiliyyah*, which in Arabic means "ignorance," or more specifically, "ignorance of God." One could expect this kind of society to be faulty, inconsistent, chaotic and unjust because man without God's guidance is unable to successfully guide himself.

All civilizations have been saturated with evidence of God's existence. In order for any person living in the modern world to be truly ignorant of God or religion, he would have to have been denied contact with the media, communication devices, educational facilities, the arts and printed word.

> *"Those who do not know say, 'Why does Allah not speak to us or there come to us a sign?' Thus spoke those before them like their words. Their hearts resemble each other. We have shown clearly the signs to a people who are certain [in faith].'"*[77]
>
> *"But those who deny Our verses are deaf and dumb within darknesses. Whomever Allah wills –*

---

[76]*Islam Between East and West*, p. 45.
[77]*Surah al-Baqarah*, 2:118.

*He leaves astray; and whomever He wills – He puts him on a straight path.*"[78]

Culture is all around us. It is most resplendently evident in architectural designs throughout the ages. Of particular beauty are places of worship. Ancient cathedrals, blue tiled mosques, and churches with soaring steeples bear testimony to the fact that mankind seeks his Creator. With such reminders man is confronted by the concept of God. He is faced with the need to make a decision and reply. He has basically two choices: to acknowledge or reject.

Indeed, religion has permeated the planet. But in the modern world, man rarely acknowledges it. This is possibly due to an arrogant and false sense of self-sufficiency. As humans progress, making leaps and bounds in science, for example, the idea of religion becomes like an outdated fairy tale to many people. For this reason, many merely toy with religion, and many others reject it altogether.

Man's rejection and denial of religion is evident. Although the airways and television are full of religious programming, they make little impact on man's spiritual void because he is offended by the idea of being sold a religion. Why does he not make a choice? Is it because he cannot buy any of the religions being promoted? And if this is so, then he must ask himself, "Where is the religion of God?" The marketplace in which religion is being peddled has made intelligent people skeptical of religion in general. They are left confused and can see no viable alternative to what is being offered.

The general priorities of people today are far from what religion requires of individuals. Most are extremely centered on themselves, on competition, on success in worldly affairs, and on the temporary comforts offered by material wealth.

---

[78]*Surah al-An'am,* 6:39.

Contemporary man has a voracity for pleasure and longs for the "good life."[79] He longs to fill the void and find comfort, but he does not find it through these means. Man is not ignorant of religion, he is negligent of it. Bereft of religion, whatever solace he finds, he finds only within himself.

The need man has for religion and guidance is not a myth. Without religion he has no grounding or base where he can find balance, peace, and authentic liberation. True religion is akin to an anchor. When grasped, it keeps one stable, unwavering and prevents drifting from one ideology, lifestyle or cult to another. True religion cannot be merely a way of thinking about life; it must be a way of living by sure guidance. With true religion man's morality becomes steadfast and unchangeable. He is responsible to God – the only one worthy of worship and obedience. At once, this also changes man's attitude toward other people and the way he feels about himself.

*"And Allah would not let a people stray after He has guided them until He makes clear to them what they should avoid. Indeed, Allah is Knowing of all things."*[80]

*"And when affliction touches man, he calls upon Us, whether lying on his side or sitting or standing; but when We remove from him his affliction, he continues [in disobedience] as if he had never called upon Us to [remove] an affliction that touched him. Thus it is made pleasing to the transgressors that which they have been doing."*[81]

---

[79] It is not only contemporary man who longs for the "good life." Countless people in the past were destroyed by their lusts and desires. Ed.
[80] *Surah at-Tawbah,* 9:115.
[81] *Surah Yunus,* 10:12.

As humanity has reached the second millennium, religion is needed more urgently than ever. As Western civilization lurches ahead more automated, mechanized and computerized, it has lost touch with human nature. Mankind is becoming dehumanized.

## Morality Comes Only from Religion

Religion is the source from which morality springs. Without religion as a basis for morality, people attempt to create their own morality. They decide for themselves what is appropriate and what is not, what is moral and what is not, etc. However, there is a vast difference between religious morality and manmade morality. People who do not follow any religion gather ideas of what is right and wrong from psychology, philosophy, popular cultural trends, and even other people. In today's modern cultures liberalized minds promote the idea that as mankind progresses into the future, religion may also be manipulated and changed by the hands of man in order to keep up with the times. At that point, morality becomes a free-for-all. Few know or even care about truth because they have become gods unto themselves, decreeing right and wrong according to their slavish desires. As a result, anything can be justified, and the imploding of society as we know it is not far away.

Such indications are evident within most world religions today. Where the Catholic Church once held strict convictions about divorce and abortion, it has now liberalized its stance on these and other issues. Christians today are vastly divided, not only through their numerous denominations but over many important moral issues, such as alcohol use, usury and taxation, abortion, divorce, and the interpretation of "the Holy Spirit." Since most of the world's religions are evolving due to man's changes, most people who have an identified religion have become not much different from those who have devised their own morality.

Indeed, mankind is in a serious state of spiritual void while unaware of its depth.

> *"Say, 'O People of the Scripture, do not exceed limits in your religion beyond the truth and do not follow the inclinations of a people who had gone astray before and misled many and have strayed from the soundness of the way.'"*[82]

Although various definitions of morality presently exist, people still share many of the same values and beliefs as to what is right and wrong. In childhood most morality is a direct outcome of upbringing. The culture in which one is brought up has an especially great influence. However, there are fundamental morals which are common to almost every society. For example, most people agree that to commit murder, practice incest, or steal is morally wrong. But then there are other issues, such as the drinking of alcohol, over which people disagree. While some feel alcohol is a moral issue, others do not. This gives rise to other questions. Does one base his decision on whether or not to drink alcohol on a moral basis or on a health perspective? Some people believe that health issues are also moral issues. The point is that what one person feels is right another might feel is wrong. This ultimately leaves one with the question of who is right.

> *"And [for] every person We have imposed his fate upon his neck, and We will produce for him on the Day of Resurrection a record which he will encounter spread open. [It will be said], 'Read your record. Sufficient is yourself against you this Day as accountant.'"*[83]

Indeed, man has been created with freedom. He has the freedom to choose between belief or unbelief, and he can

---

[82] *Surah al-Ma'idah*, 5:77.
[83] *Surah al-Isra'*, 17:13-14.

freely pursue what he considers to be right or wrong. He can even choose from among many different religions, although it can be deduced through human intelligence that if there is a God, there can only be one true God. And if there is one God, there must only be one ordained way of life. There cannot logically be two differing ways of life intended by the Creator. Therefore, and emphatically, there *is* a right and wrong way.

When man does not make an outright commitment towards finding God's way, he must then depend upon his own limited knowledge to decide what he will define as right and wrong. The result of one human thinking process can be seen in satanic cult members and their rituals. These people have decided through their own reasoning that there is some benefit to the worship of Satan; otherwise, they would not be doing it. They feel that what they are doing is good. But when satanic cult members perform human sacrifices (something they consider to be of value), most condemn it as a waste of human life. Through this one realizes more thoroughly that morality means different things to different people – a fact that should make one certain he is indeed in need of guidance.

*"And say, 'The truth is from your Lord, so whoever wills – let him believe; and whoever wills – let him disbelieve.'"*[84]

Morality is always prohibitive.[85] For example, eight of the Ten Commandments are restrictions on human behavior.[86] Almost everyone knows the exhortations: "thou shall not kill," "thou shall not commit adultery," and "thou shall not steal." Most religious people agree that mankind is in need of some sort of guidelines and restrictions, or else they would not be

---

[84]*Surah al-Kahf,* 18:29.
[85]*Islam Between East and West,* p. 122.
[86]Ibid., p. 122.

able to commit themselves to their religions. But there are other people who are on a quest to find unlimited freedom. The reality of religious morality, however, is that the prohibitions sent from God partially sanctioning human nature are vitally necessary. They prevent man from harming himself and others and prevent him from creating unjust systems. Therefore, such prohibitions cannot be considered wrong or oppressive because they serve a purpose. Divine prohibitions are not meant to curtail human freedom; rather, they define and dignify human freedom.

## Man Is Unable to Guide Himself

Within civilization man is surrounded by others like himself, and he finds that he shares much in common with his fellow men. Humans are similar and share the same basic needs. Mankind endlessly pursues that which offers pleasure and flees from whatever threatens to cause pain. The "fight or flight" instinct is always at work to protect one from physical, mental and emotional harm. What one does in response to that instinct is largely dependent upon his moral standards. As Yusef Islam (former pop-singer Cat Stevens) said, "When we are hurting, we look for something to comfort us."[87] Therefore, people have a tendency to assume that things which comfort or bring pleasure are good, while they consider all that causes pain to be evil.[88] But here is where the distinctions between people are clarified. When in trouble, the religious man turns to God, but the one without religion runs from the pain and turns to something else (like alcohol), which will take his attention away from whatever is bothering him. Here are two people with the same needs and same affliction but who seek different means by which to find comfort.

---

[87]VCR entitled, *Why I am a Muslim,* 3rd Annual Convention, Dayton, Ohio, Oct. 31-Sept. 3, 1984.
[88]*Islam Between East and West,* p. 126.

Man has been endowed with great mental capacity. However, it is not sufficient to guide him in this life nor to steer him clear from certain errors. Modern science has failed to unlock all the mysteries of life. The most brilliant pioneers of science who created a nuclear bomb powerful enough to blow up the earth several times over are unable to unlock the secrets of human existence. The French scientist, André Lwoff, said that man is still unable to create[89] a single living organism, and he cannot even produce one living bacteria.[90] Although medical science has failed thus far to unravel the unknown mechanisms of the human brain, it continues to observe qualities in the human body that are no less miraculous. For example, the tear of the human eye contains the strongest bactericide found in any pharmaceutical drug and can destroy up to one hundred different kinds of bacteria – even when diluted many times.[91] Man's intelligence brings him very close to the knowledge he needs to understand life, but even so, he does not always use it in the right way. For example, research proves that alcohol kills brain cells when consumed even in small amounts. Scientific evidence also shows that brain cells do not regenerate. So why do so many people still drink alcohol? It would seem not due to lack of knowledge but more for the need to escape. What causes man to seek self-destructive outlets to banish sadness, boredom and the like? Could it be that without proper religious grounding mankind becomes easily jarred by life's forces?

The simile used in previous paragraphs likening religion to an anchor is made crystal clear here. The stability offered in cyclonic "soul storms" of temptation, depression, lack of self-worth, and infinitum is quite real. If the human soul is "anchored" to the Truth, it will weather whatever the

---

[89]Creation in the literal sense of origination, not reproduction.
[90]*Islam Between East and West,* p. 23.
[91]Ibid., p. 25.

seas of life may toss at it. Knowledge of the true way to live will free human beings from the false, fleeting traps that promise comfort and escape.

## The Jahiliyyah Society

The *jahiliyyah* civilization of pre-Islamic Arabia was a life lived without true religion. The absence of religious values caused people to fall into immoral, even bestial behaviors. Ironically, many of those pagan customs are akin to what modern man resorts to when he is void of religion, morality, and God – he lives as he pleases. The pagan Arabs were no different; they wanted to do whatever made them feel good.

Pre-Islamic pagan Arabia was not blessed by the influence of religion. For a long time the people had lived in a remote land, isolated from civilization, living their lives by manmade laws. Because of the peninsula's geographic isolation, its people had little contact with other cultures who had once been enlightened by revelation, e.g., the early Jews or Christians. The Arab inhabitants of this isolated portion of land were firm traditionalists, steeped in superstition, and devoted to idol worship.

It is a significant aspect of man that he possesses the instinctive need to worship something. Man is not, as some have claimed, "an intelligent animal." Rather, he is an entirely different species. Only man fashions idols and statues for worship. Only man stares up at the stars and looks deeply into the face of the moon. Only man feels wonder and awe and is stunned by the beauty and complexity of life. Only man feels an urge to bow and prostrate himself before a being greater than himself.

How do we explain this? Certainly, it is not a result of his learned intelligence or understanding of life. It is the human instinct to worship, to seek and find God which emanates naturally from within. It is also evident that if this need to worship is ignored or suppressed, it invariably manifests itself in deviant ways. Examples include modern cults founded in America, from the "Moonies" to the "Davidians." People go to great lengths to seek out something to believe in and worship. Jim Jones' worshippers committed mass suicide together with their leader (or "messiah") at his command by drinking cyanide-laced Kool-Aid. Numerous satanic cults thrive throughout the United States.

The pagan Arabs had many gods. They worshipped everything from statues to stars and were accustomed to very unusual rituals. Although one might view the rituals as ludicrous or inhumane, it cannot be denied that many of their practices resemble those of modern-day cults and other lifestyles. Their morality, as one would expect, was quite low. Their tribes were anything but peaceful retreats. Wars, vengeance and murder were rampant. Basically, the pre-Islamic Arabs were free – so free that they could do almost anything they wanted to do. Each man took justice into his own hands, which usually resulted in further wrongdoing.

Girls were thought to be burdensome and a source of shame. If a woman gave birth to a baby girl, the family felt free to reject the baby and might bury her alive. However, great value was placed on the birth of a male, for he would help the family as he grew older. The lives of women at that time were especially filled with injustice, abuse and oppression. Rape was rampant. Women were treated like slaves and had no human rights to inheritance or other financial means. Most went into marriage without any personal property. They were at the complete mercy of their husbands – men who indulged in intoxicants, gambling and adultery.

In earlier civilizations after divine revelations were sent through the prophets, their interpretations were altered by men. Under the banner of Christianity, for example, women were said to be evil, more likely to fall into sin, and were not to be trusted because they could tempt a man into the depths of darkness. There was also speculation that they had no souls. The Church blamed Eve for the temptation that took place in the garden, and through this women's dignity as human beings was thwarted. They would, for many centuries to follow, be thought of as evil, necessitating control by men.

The mercy of God and His promise to not leave mankind to wander without guidance was fulfilled periodically when He sent prophets. However, there were still people who stubbornly clung to their former ways and refused belief. Every prophet gave mankind the same message: "O mankind, worship God. You have no other deity but Him."[92] But many of the idol worshippers continued to worship their manmade statues anyway. Nothing seemed to penetrate their minds. Long after Prophets Abraham and Ishmael erected the Holy *Ka'bah* for the worship of God alone, pagan idol worshippers filled it with their statues. They also circled the *Ka'bah* and paraded throughout this place of worship in immoral and disrespectful ways. Their idol worship did not change their character; they were still ignorant, unguided and degenerate.

## The Prophet of Islam

God's mercy and forbearance toward His creation is most evident when into this dark and evil time He sent the last of the prophets, Muhammad (ﷺ), who had been prophesied by Jesus. The Arabian Peninsula, not far from the land where Jesus had preached, was where God sent His last messenger. The story of Prophet Muhammad's early years is a sad one. In his youth he experienced emotional

---

[92]See Qur'anic verses 7:59, 7:65, 7:73, 7:85, 11:50, 11:61, 11:84, 23:23, and 23:32.

pain and endured personal disappointments. After both of his parents had died, he went to live with his grandfather, but shortly thereafter, he, too, passed away. As custom had it, Muhammad (ﷺ) then became a ward of his uncle.

Prophet Muhammad (ﷺ) belonged to the tribe of Quraysh. He raised sheep, remained unlettered, and had practically no exposure to other peoples. He was raised within the *jahiliyyah* society. Oddly enough, despite all of his unfortunate circumstances, he remained true to his inborn nature (*fitrah*) and was not duly influenced by the people around him. He was known to be polite, honest, just and fair in business dealings, and as a young man, people referred to him as "*al-Ameen*" (Arabic for "the Trustworthy"). Prophet Muhammad (ﷺ) was generous, noble, and avoided strife, remaining unscathed by the corruption and violence around him.

Years later as an adult, Muhammad (ﷺ) came to feel great distaste at the way people were leading their lives. He was repelled by what he saw in idol worship as the degradation of humanity and the darkness of evil around him. He felt a need to retreat and often departed into the hills, isolating himself in want of peace, solitude and guidance. He sought answers and reflected on what he knew about life, longing to know the truth.

It was in a cave that God spoke to him through the angel, Gabriel. The first revealed word was "read" (also translated as "recite"). Muhammad (ﷺ) was naturally shaken by this experience and went directly to his beloved wife, Khadijah, to tell her what had happened to him. From her reaction one can see that his relationship with Khadijah was special. She was the one he wanted to tell of Gabriel's visit. And it was she who comforted and reassured him he had not lost his senses, confirming to him that he had been chosen by God for prophethood.

Prophet Muhammad (ﷺ) drove the message home when he reminded the people that although man may deceive his fellow man, he cannot deceive God. The Prophet (ﷺ) continued despite the fact that the inhabitants of his homeland were increasingly incited by his words. Nonetheless, he kept spreading the message until nearly all of the Arabian Peninsula had submitted to God alone. He did it without a great military force, without prior military training, without sophisticated weaponry or man power. Only by the power of God could such a man in such short time become such a successful leader. Many non-Muslims worldwide credit Prophet Muhammad (ﷺ) for his leadership ability and astounding brilliance as a strategist. The Encyclopedia Britannica states, "Muhammed is the most successful of all prophets and religious personalities."[93]

Indeed, Prophet Muhammad (ﷺ) was a commander, businessman, preacher, statesman, judge, spiritual reformer, protector of slaves, and emancipator of women. All of this, and he was neither trained in education, military leadership, social reform or law, nor did he receive any other special training that would have enabled him to succeed. But God enabled him in order to make His message known to mankind.

## Islam Freed the Pagans

Once revealed in its entirety the Qur'anic message drastically altered the lives of everyone, especially women, who had been sadly oppressed and abused. Fourteen hundred years ago women experienced the most wonderfully liberating revolution known in all of world history. It was without a doubt the most positively enlightening revolution ever – not just for women but all mankind. For the first time women were granted equality, granted their dignity, and

---

[93]Vol. 11.

were legally protected from abusive ideologies. As they progressed and followed the divine revelation, women realized for the first time how it felt to be respected, dignified and equal in worth. Islam not only emancipated people from idol worship, it emancipated them from servitude to manmade systems. Suddenly, women had an equal standing with men as human beings in society. Islam brought a complete code of morality, addressing every component of life necessary for peace, health and happiness. Through God's guidance, men become responsible and trustworthy, and women become dignified members of society.

The impact of Islam not only touched the lives of women but affected all people. Many Christians and Jews sought refuge during the Islamic expansion from the ethnocentrism and legalism which the priests and rabbis promulgated. Christian monks were released from self-imposed celibacy. Islam freed pious worshippers from the inhumane entrapments of isolation, loneliness, superstition, and devotion to things that could not help them. Once the entire revelation was known throughout Arabia, people began to understand that there is a balance between the material and spiritual worlds: that both men and women belong to God and that each has a specific ordained role during his/her term of trial on earth.

*"And it is He who has made you successors upon the earth and has raised some of you above others in degrees [of rank] that He may try you through what He has given you. Indeed, your Lord is swift in penalty; but indeed, He is Forgiving and Merciful."*[94]

There exists no greater example to the depths man can sink when in the state of degeneration void of guidance, and

---

[94] *Surah al-An'am,* 6:165.

to the heights the human personality can reach when under the influence of religion, as has been witnessed in the powerful transformation of pagan Arabia. What is certain is that within either of these conditions, man will find nothing to stop him from either soaring to the highest height or from sinking to the lowest low accept one thing – his free choice.

# We Are Equal, but We Are Not the Same

## Towards Androgyny

When Islam freed the pagans, equality between men and women was established. But somehow, somewhere, women in the West lost the true meanings of "equality" and "liberation." As a result, there began a movement whose goal was to have women treated and thought of "the same" as men – no distinctions, no discrimination. This demand is not compatible with a woman's physical or spiritual nature. Because she is created in many ways distinctly different[95] than a man, modern women want to diminish the impact of these differences. This is an alarming sign that something is quite amiss. Women are not living their lives the way they are entitled, and they do not want to admit having any limitations nor admit their vulnerabilities as women. However, irregardless of how much legislation has passed to treat women the same as men, one fact will remain eternally unchanged: the female gender was created with different needs and capabilities than that of the male. Not less, not substandard, not lacking – just different. Simply put, a woman and a man should complement each other: ideally, they complete each other in marriage.

If feminists achieve their goal to be like men, it will force them to alter their true nature. When they reach the plateau, there will be androgyny. The signs of this are predominantly seen in Western societies where women are dressing and behaving aggressively, even "manly," to prove themselves.

---

[95]Feminists have successfully implanted the concept of "different" meaning "less."

Major differences between men and women should be mentioned to establish a groundwork. First and by far the most major difference between men and women is the fact that the male human is physically stronger than the female. Men simply have a much larger muscle mass than women. Additionally, their bones are larger. Women are usually smaller framed, and they have more fat on their bodies. Women and men differ in their hormonal chemistry. These chemicals not only affect personality traits but can also alter the emotions and cognitive functions of the brain. Hormone levels vary between men and women, and they have different kinds of hormones and chemistry makeup. A man's hormones remain more steady, while women's hormones tend to fluctuate throughout their lifetime, especially during menstruation, pregnancy, postpartum, and menopause. During these times, women can experience swings in body weight, moods and physical stamina. For example, some women experience menstrual periods that are quite debilitating. Most women experience some physical, emotional or mental symptoms related to hormonal fluctuations at this time, and to varying degrees, all women experience some stress-related fatigue or irritability. The condition is so widespread that the medical community coined the term PMS (premenstrual syndrome). In America, courts of law now recognize this syndrome as a precursor to some violent and even bizarre acts committed by women. In fact, women have used PMS as part of their defense strategy in court. The attention and approval from the courts regarding these defense motions created quite a stir among both sexes. Certainly, feminists opposed the courts validating this significant gender difference. At the same time, many men railed against the idea that women should be prosecuted differently because of their hormonal fluctuations. The undeniable fact remains that women are using their physical differences to their advantage in these cases.

Postpartum depression is another physical condition exclusive to the female gender. For some women postpartum depression can develop a few days or even months after child birth. Defense lawyers argue that this postnatal depression caused their clients to kill or endanger the lives of their newborns.

Pregnancy is, of course, another major difference between men and women. Pregnancy, childbirth and childrearing is not only physically and emotionally challenging, it is a full-time job. It is also the most significant difference among men and women in terms of role playing. This is the dividing line separating men from women. Pregnancy alters a woman's life dramatically. It is not an easy task. For one, pregnancy is often a confining period which slows down the body to varying degrees. Women should be given time to recuperate after the birth and given time to care for their baby in a safe, peaceful and supportive family environment.

The differences between men and women do not end here. Men and women are not sexually oriented in quite the same way either. Very simply, due to his anatomy and physical strength a man is able to force sex upon a woman, but most women cannot force a man into having sexual intercourse. Therefore, women are more vulnerable to sexual harassment. Can most women physically or sexually threaten a man? Can most women break into a man's house, physically overpower him and then molest or rape him? The answer is obvious.

Another often ignored difference existing between females and males are the ways they are sexually aroused. Studies conducted by behaviorists, psychologists and sociologists have concluded that men are sexually stimulated primarily by visual stimuli. This could explain why men are more gratified by pornographic material than women. In fact, the entire pornography industry (from publications, female strip shows, topless bars and pornographic films) is male-dominated, that is, men produce it for men. Unfortunately, it is women who voluntarily contribute to the success of the pornography empire by debasing themselves in print, film, etc. Although Muslim women have been modest and chaste to ensure their protection and dignity for the past 1400 years, it is interesting that modern-day psychologists are now "discovering" the power of visual sexual stimuli for men and advising women to dress appropriately to avoid "possible problems."

There also exist fundamental core differences in the ways men and women experience life. Women will admit inferiority to men when it is convenient and profitable to do so. For example, in professional sports or at the Olympics, women willingly do not compete in the same sport against men. Conversely, women demand and sue for entrance into the Citadel, a once all-male military academy in South Carolina. Although these women might pass the academic entrance exams, physical endurance tests, etc., there seems no cause for celebration. Most people object to seeing their husbands or sons drafted for military duty. And now, mothers, daughters, nieces and aunts are being drafted as well.

This quest for equality resembles other demands from women to be treated the same as men but which enslaves them to the system. It does not promote the family unit, marriage, or the woman's role as nurturer for her children. Will women be segregated on the battlefield so they will not be raped and pillaged by their own comrades? Further along these lines, it can be predicted that when a female infantry is seized, female prisoners of war will certainly give war a new meaning. They will undoubtedly become victims of the enemy camp. Will her training, physical ability and guns help her then?

Overall, the differences between men and women and the impact they have on women is astounding. Why these issues continue to be brushed aside is unbelievably degrading and even dangerous for women.

## Islam – The Key to Human Liberation

Islam's purpose is to guide mankind to a way of life which strikes a balance between the physical and spiritual worlds. Islamic laws, if followed properly, will meet this requirement in a complete and fulfilling manner. Along these lines, Muslim writer Hammudah Abdalati has stated succinctly, "When a civilized people abide by the laws of their countries, they are considered sound citizens and honest members of their respective societies. No responsible person would say that such people lose their freedom by their obedience to the law. No rational being would think or believe for a moment that such law-abiding people are fatalists and helpless. Similarly, the person who submits to the will of God, which is a good will, and obeys the law of God, which is the best law, is a sound and honest person... Submission to the good will of God, therefore, does not take away or curtail individual freedom."[96]

So what is the truth about the mysterious Muslim woman behind the veil? Is she fulfilled? Is she oppressed? And in what ways do she and her culture compare and contrast to her Western counterpart? As has been seen, many misconceptions about Islam are creations of numerous forces and factors. Some are innocent, some not. Now more than ever there is a fear and mistrust of Muslims and Islam alike. Most Westerners know nothing or very little about Islam. Many of the assumptions they have are wrong. The public laps up sensationalized stories about the "tortured and oppressed" women of Islam. They say that Muslim women are subjected to cruelty by their families and husbands and that their lives are inhumanely limited to the running of the

---

[96] *Islam in Focus*, p. 8.

household and to the raising of numerous children. According to the authentic sources of Islam,[97] there is no truth to any of these statements, and, in fact, every one of them is false.

From the Islamic perspective nearly everything that is currently happening in Western culture that is problematic (even from the Westerner's point of view) is the direct outcome of man's insistence on eschewing guidance and responsibility for one's actions. Cleared of responsibility, man descends morally lower than creatures in the animal kingdom. Such people abhor anything which threatens to restrict their progression towards absolute and unlimited freedom. People in the Western world have been brainwashed into believing that guidelines, even if beneficial for the individual and society, are evil, restrictive, and even inhumane. As ridiculous as this sounds, it is the modern mind-set in the West, especially of the new generation. They classify the gain of such "freedoms" as obtainment of "human rights." Even some of the most intelligent, progressive people are not able to see the error in this type of thinking. Their misinterpretation of what it is to be free surely promises tribulation and further human degradation for the whole society, especially in the areas of morality, crime and human spirituality.

One of Islam's first tenets is "let there be no compulsion in religion."[98] This means that religious beliefs, conviction or acceptance cannot be forced upon a single person or mass of people. Therefore, it is in this context that religion is discussed as an attempt to clarify, explain and invite one to listen, thereby giving total human freedom to accept or reject by one's own choice.

---

[97]The Qur'an, authentic *hadith* (sayings of Prophet Muhammad), and *shari'ah* (Islamic law).
[98]See *Surah al-Baqarah*, 2:256.

Islam also addresses man's imperfection and fallibility. The Creator has not left His creation to wander about without guidance. Allah's revelation, when applied, will guide one to the highest possible level of perfection for mankind. However, this does not imply that man, even in a state of submission to God, will reach total perfection or will never commit a mistake or error. It means that if followed as prescribed, Islam can help man and human civilizations achieve the highest level of dignity and liberation for both men and women. Being imperfect or fallible is not a sin according to Islam, for to err is human.

In order for people to have human dignity, both men and women must be allowed to be as Allah intended – free to be themselves. In order for this to take place, there must be a fundamental foundation which begins with the equality of men and women. In order for the two sexes to come together harmoniously and naturally, it must be understood that they are identical in value as human beings. But "equality" cannot be equated to mean "the same" because men and women are not the same in many physical and emotional aspects. Islam addresses the issues of equality by telling mankind:

*"O mankind, fear your Lord, who created you from one soul and created from it its mate and dispersed from both of them many men and women. And fear Allah, through whom you ask one another, and the wombs. Indeed Allah is ever, over you, an Observer."*[99]

It is clear that Islam confirms equality between the sexes. Men and women were given mutual rights. For this reason there is no longer a need for competition between the sexes. Islam rectifies and clarifies the human personality and the identities of men and women and places them on equal ground as to worth, importance, intelligence and rights.

---

[99] *Surah an-Nisa'*, 4:1.

## Islam – Empowerment to Be One's True Self

Although much has been said by the media about Islam, perhaps the veil can be lifted which has kept the West from understanding what Islam is really about. Islam affirms the equality of the sexes, but it clearly steers mankind away from assuming that men and women are the same. The most significant difference between Islamic and Western outlooks is that Islam recognizes the differences between men and women, therefore treating each individually. Islam sets a firm foundation for how the two sexes should think of themselves and each other. Thus, due to the obvious differences between men and women, Islam exhorts men to be the protectors of women:

*"Men are in charge of women by [right of] what [qualities] Allah has given one over the other and what they spend [for maintenance] from their wealth."*[100]

The significance of this ordinance cannot be diminished. It is a tremendous liberation for women. When this distinction is fully understood, it cannot in any way be interpreted negatively. It does not mean that women become the property or possessions of men. It does not mean that women are frail, incapable, weak-minded or unable to accomplish anything of great value. It simply confronts women's needs and guarantees their right to maintenance as wives, daughters or mothers.

Islam affirms that women, with their particular physical anatomy, are in need of special consideration and protection. It exhorts Muslim men to treat their mothers, sisters, wives and other female relations in a responsible, loving, and yes, protective way. Women who travel or live alone are easy targets in any type of setting. When Muslim women travel,

---

[100]*Surah an-Nisa'*, 4:34.

they are accompanied by their husband or other close male relative. Countless crimes have happened in the West when a woman was alone for only minutes within her own neighborhood. She was stalked, abducted, raped and killed without a trail of evidence. The stalker out of sight and free. High profile people like actors or actresses never go out of their houses alone for fear of being attacked or just harassed. Crazed people do not usually go for difficult targets who are surrounded by others, and especially who are being escorted by a man. In the West violence against women is a growing major issue and threat. Women are victims of domestic abuse, rape and other sexual assaults, which are happening more and more routinely. Many women have literally been abandoned by their fathers, brothers and husbands. The statistics of rape, beatings, unwelcomed sexual advances, etc. abound. Until men (and women!) admit and accept the fact that women are being used and abused by the present Western mindset, real liberation will remain a confused dream.

Furthermore, Islam addresses another vital issue – that of modesty. Modesty is not only a way of thinking. Modesty is an active, living virtue as opposed to the mere philosophy of dignified, respectable men and women. Without this moral accountability, society is sure to fall prey to various kinds of base, lewd behavior. Islamic revelation tells mankind that all people have a responsibility to society. And all are warned that sexually permissive acts are the beginning of a downward spiritual and physical spiral that threatens the very fiber of a decent, civilized people. The negative consequences of permissiveness and immodesty (among them: disease, physical abuse, broken families, substance abuse, crime, and illegitimate babies) are the very factors that continue to enslave the human spirit. Islam calls to liberate mankind from this devilish deception.

As stated earlier, modesty demands active means, not limited only to one's outer dress, but inclusive of interaction between the sexes. The following Qur'anic injunction explains:

> *"Tell the believing men to reduce some of their vision[101] and guard their private parts.[102] That is purer for them. Indeed, Allah is Acquainted with what they do. And tell the believing women to reduce some of their vision and guard their private parts and not display their adornment[103] except that which [ordinarily] appears thereof[104] and to draw their headcovers over their chests and not display their adornment [i.e., beauty] except to..."*[105]

Here an exhortation is given to both men and women to guard their chastity. Islam especially calls women to cover their beauty and not use it as a means of attracting attention, for that is comparable to a prostitute soliciting her wares. Men and women are both told to limit their gaze. This does not mean that they must go about with their eyes cast down but means that they must exercise control over their passions and to refrain from staring at the opposite sex in public places or eliciting undue attention. Prophet Muhammad (ﷺ) said that to glance at a woman once is excused but to look a second time is a sin. Contrastingly, non-Muslims tend to initially choose their perspective partners by first "checking out" the other's physical beauty. The family structure no longer takes part in bringing young people together for marriage. In the past both American and European families would take part in finding a man for their daughters to marry, and vice versa. Now, people in Western societies

---

[101]Looking only at what is lawful and averting their eyes from what is unlawful.
[102]From being seen and from unlawful acts.
[103]Both natural beauty, such as hair or body shape, and that with which a woman beautifies herself of clothing, jewelry, etc.
[104]i.e., the outer garments or whatever might appear out of necessity.
[105]*Surah an-Nur*, 24:30-31.

tend to remain single longer and spend many years looking and trying out their perspective partners.

Clearly, many problems associated with women which are now being addressed by concerned, professional people can be directly related to how women are trying to live their lives just like men. Their culture has denied them their right to be women. Some questions need to be asked: Why are women in the West being valued merely as sex objects? Why are they being raped and assaulted? Why are they the victims while men rarely are? This is easily understood from an Islamic perspective because Muslim women are not left out in society to fend for themselves. The structure of Western society has given men license to abuse, manipulate and brainwash, and women have the liberty to experience this abuse. And the West does not consider this oppressive? Indeed, it is a manmade system which is unjust and degrading to women.

Is it fair to expect, force or request one or both of the sexes to suppress, change or deny their God-given differences in order to selfishly structure a human society? Why is this not considered a human rights issue? Does it not deny women their rights to womanhood, family and motherhood? In contrast, Islam cannot be manipulative in regards to true human nature because it acknowledges and respects the differences between men and women. Islamic society is an environment whereby both sexes are considered equal in worth and are free to be themselves. Islam exhorts men and women to behave in specific ways which protects women from abuse and denies men the right to abuse. This is not oppression. This is the outstretched hand that has been offered to women for over fourteen hundred years.

## Western Degradation of the Woman

Scholar and author, Camille Paglia, optimized the Western degradation of the woman when she wrote in a college text about contemporary issues, "Western culture has a roving eye. Male sex is hunting and scanning: boys hang yelping from honking cars, acting like jerks over strolling girls; men lunching on girders go through the primitive book of wolf whistles and animal clucks. Everywhere, the beautiful woman is scrutinized and harassed. She is the ultimate symbol of human desire. The feminine is that-which-is-sought; it recedes beyond our grasp. Hence, there is always a feminine element in the beautiful young man of male homosexuality. The feminine is ever-elusive, a silver shimmer on the horizon... Islam is wise to drape women in black, for the eye is the avenue of Eros..."[106]

It is surprising and pleasing to see that a non-Muslim has broken through the barrier and grasped a very important Islamic principle which addresses the differences between men and women. She especially emphasizes that beautiful women in the West are sought after and have become the "ultimate symbol" of human desire and that the male has a "roving eye," forever "scanning" and "hunting" for the woman who makes herself more visible in the public eye. She concludes that the draping of women in Islam "is wise... for the eye is the avenue of Eros," meaning eroticism or sexual desire but not necessarily love.

How has such degradation happened? How can women preserve their dignity in such a society? Is it not clear that intermingling of men and women at all levels of society is at the forefront of the problem and that women are being harassed as a result? It is not difficult to see with a quick glance the casual ways in which men feel at liberty to approach, harass and devalue women. Consequently, in response, women value themselves in much the same way. Why are men so intent and fixed upon scanning the public for women, especially beautiful women? More importantly,

---

[106]Camille Paglia, "Sexual Aggression and Nature," *Sexual Harassment – Confrontations and Decisions,* p. 119.

how has this affected the women of that society? Why do women continue to tolerate it by playing the game? More interestingly, while men rate women according to their size, shape and beauty, why do women continue to dress the part in order to attract more attention instead of resisting the urge to conform? Why are women so willing to be leered at as sex objects and valued only for their looks instead of who they are on the inside? It is devaluing to be sure. Many Western women have become numb and desensitized to this issue and do not realize that their own actions have drastically reduced their status. Perhaps they no longer think of it as degrading. For sure, many women play the game well and even go to great lengths to appear in public in the most ludicrous hair, makeup and fashion, almost screaming "look at me!" What do they gain from this attention by strange men in the society? Is it approval? Self-esteem? Indeed, such women are approval seekers in dire need of *real* self-esteem. Thus, it is clear how civilization has reached its zenith in demoting the woman from a human being to nothing more than an object.

## Sex Objects, Immorality, and Rampant Divorce

It has often been asserted that Islam is a religion of extremism. Yet, in all fairness, the same can be said of Western culture when seen from an Islamic perspective. The two systems demonstrate very different ways of life, but this does not necessarily mean that they have totally different values. An Islamic society is structured to obtain what many Western people believe in and value but what they are unable to achieve through the way their society is structured. Many relationships in the West are treated as casual interludes. This casualness has allowed women to be degraded and men to be abusive. This is seen not only in Hollywood, in modeling, and on television but also in the workplace. The importance of the woman's personality and character has been taken away and replaced with something else – her appearance. Most significantly, there has emerged a society of people set free from morality. No one should wonder why this society is so divorce ridden. Although reasons for divorce vary, one study highlights the distinct difference between Islamic societies (where strong, closely knit family structures are the norm) and Western-style families. "A new study shows the risk of divorce or separation goes up for young married couples in the United States if they live in an area with plenty of unmarried and available men or women. That suggests many husbands and wives keep an eye out for a better partner..." researcher Scott J. South says. "The more possibilities they see, the better the chance of finding someone worth leaving the marriage for..." He assumes unhappy marriages are especially vulnerable, but he could not rule out some effect on people quite satisfied with their marriages who happen to meet the partner of their dreams.[107]

This gives rise to the notion that in societies where casual sexual relationships are condoned and where women and men mix freely that this could cause the likelihood of divorce to escalate drastically. While some divorces occur because the two people have simply grown apart, the study suggests that in a "liberated" society marriage breakups are a result of cultural instability and societal pressures.

Furthermore, it seems reasonable to expect that men will have busier eyes when women are on parade in public, dressing in order to garner attention. The inclination for men to gaze is within their nature and is not something that will go away or change. Men will not one day wake up and have a new sexual orientation, nor will they become magically desensitized to women. The way in which women dress can

---

[107]"Couples Officially Warned of Marriage Hazards," *Arab News*; Feb. 18, 1995; study also appeared in a monthly issue of the *American Sociological Review*.

either deter this inclination in men or can heighten and even instigate unwanted attention from men. Today, Western men are quite literally saturated by visual stimuli at every turn. Sex and sensuality is a dominating theme. Whether in the workplace, in public, or on the TV screen, sex is everywhere.

# Freedom to Be Undressed

## In the West: Oppressed If You Are Dressed

Although human beings share the same basic needs and desires, the planet is nonetheless filled with diverse customs, traditions, and religious beliefs. When so many differences exist in any given society, it will surely create disunity, confusion, and injustice for many people. Very recently, an issue has been raised in a country that claims to be "tolerant"; however, its citizens, specifically its Muslim citizens, are not being granted their constitutional rights. As recently as 1994, Muslim school girls in France were banned from attending school because they were wearing the *hijab* (headscarf).[108] Does it not seem ironic that while women are allowed to go out in public wearing G-string bikinis to wash cars for money and to eat in public restaurants wearing a bikini top, Muslim girls are prevented from attending school because they want to cover their hair with a scarf? The subliminal message is that women who are provocatively undressed have more rights than women who are dressed. What kind of society is this blatant discrimination promoting? Due to their own intolerance, the French government has targeted and retracted their citizen's constitutional right – freedom of religion. More specifically, they oppress a religious community that upholds modest dress for women. How can one from a Western perspective explain this strange phenomenon to his/her child? On one hand, prostitution is legal and public nudity tolerated; yet, people who want to be fully clothed are harassed and discriminated against. Professor Lamand explains that the decision by the French Ministry of Education to ban the

---

[108]Frances Lamand, "The Head Scarves Issue in France: A Lawyer's Point of View – Ban is a Political, Not a Juridical Decision," interview by Moufti Lamis, *Arab News,* 1995.

wearing of a scarf is not necessarily because it is a sign of religious conviction but rather because the scarf is seen as being "ostentatious."[109] This leads one to believe that it sounds more like a personal opinion, and as such, would be difficult to legislate. Wearing a cross might be comparable, yet it is allowed. What if scarves were to become fashionable, i.e., a new Paris trend, would Muslim girls then be allowed to go back to school dressed in their *hijab*? Lamand disclosed that "French public opinion has a tendency to see the wearing of headscarves as the symbol of extremism," but he recalls that "a lot of French women used to cover their heads up to a few decades ago."[110] Why would anyone be offended by someone who wants to dress modestly and conservatively? Furthermore, in what way could the headscarf be considered provocative? It is certainly no more provocative than any other article of clothing that is allowed in public schools. How about if the situation was turned around and Muslim women were allowed to speak up about how they are offended by women who expose all parts of their bodies in public and in front of their husbands? Who is legislating this behavior as provocative?

It seems obvious that governmental policy for the private sector is doing all it can to curb its citizens from following anything other than whatever government policy promotes. So it can be gathered that when an individual becomes religious, he can expect most of the society to stand in his way. The fact is Muslims are neither being tolerated nor allowed to fulfill their religious obligations. The French banning of headscarves is an outright stripping of the right to practice one's religion as stated by the Declaration of Human Rights and the French constitution. Only in 1992 did the State Council of France rule that headscarves would be allowed and that students have the right to "express" their

---

[109]Ibid.
[110]Ibid.

faiths even at school. It further implied that "the *hijab* is declared to be compatible with secularism." Furthermore, the State Council maintained that public schools forbid "any kind of discrimination in the access to education on the basis of... the pupils' religious faiths and that pupils have the right to express or show their faiths at school..." However, the ruling conveniently excluded and banned the wearing of any religious sign if it is "provocative in the manner of wearing it."[111] While the ministry knew it could not blatantly come out and tell these girls they were not allowed to dress modestly, it had to rely on curbing the modest dress by attempting to diminish the impact of the *hijab* by prohibiting the scarf. While France and other Western countries proudly boast they are countries of tolerance and diversity, it is clear that the Muslims who live in these countries are not being tolerated and are even being legally bound from demonstrating their convictions of morality.[112]

Professor Lamand describes France as experiencing a wave of "Islamaphobia." He reminds us that there are 1.2 million Algerians residing in France and that since France and Algeria are neighbors, there is a fear within France due to the "rise of extremism, which they think can be exported to their country..."[113] There have been incidences of militant extremists who used violence, whereupon some Westerners – French citizens as well as Algerian "intellectuals" – were killed.[114] Thus, a fear, prejudice and misinterpretation of Islam in general were perpetuated.

---

[111] Frances Lamand, "Cultural Open-Mindedness a Must," interview by Moufti Lamis, *Arab News,* January 24, 1994, p. 13.
[112] After much opposition the French Ministry subsequently awarded the girls a monetary settlement for the infringement of their rights, and they were once again allowed to wear their *hijab*.
[113] Frances Lamand, "The Head Scarves Issue in France: A Lawyer's Point of View – Ban is a Political, Not a Juridical Decision," interview by Moufti Lamis, *Arab News,* 1995.
[114] Ibid.

At this point it is essential to address a vital issue. It is very unfortunate that there are groups who carry out violent acts under the banner of religion for self-centered reasons. People or groups doing this cannot be considered religious while they are taking innocent human life, a sacred gift from Allah. In Islam, if a person takes a single human life, it is as if he killed the whole human race:

*"Because of that, We decreed upon the Children of Israel that whoever kills a soul unless for a soul[115] or for corruption [done] in the land[116] – it is as if he had slain mankind entirely. And whoever saves one – it is as if he had saved mankind entirely."*[117]

Due to isolated violent acts and the media's quickness to exploit them to negatively project Islam, there is indeed a heightened intolerance of Muslims worldwide, especially in Western cultures where there is already little understanding about Islam. The journalist, Jean-Francois Revel, once wrote about "Islamo-terrorism," but why not call the so-called Christians in Ireland who have killed and maimed under the banner of their religion "Christiano-terrorism," Lamand inquires.[118]

## What Is Beneath the Veil?

Although the headcover (sometimes referred to by Westerners as "the veil") is part of the Muslim woman's *hijab,* the true definition of *hijab* is the covering of the woman's entire body. Specifically, this means that she

---

[115] i.e., in legal retribution for murder.
[116] i.e., that requiring the death penalty.
[117] *Surah al-Ma'idah,* 5:32.
[118] Frances Lamand, "The Head Scarves Issue in France: A Lawyer's Point of View – Ban is a Political, Not a Juridical Decision," interview by Moufti Lamis, *Arab News,* 1995.

covers everything except her face and hands.[119] Her hair and neck must be covered. The veil is actually a separate article of clothing used to cover the woman's face. The believers are directed thus in the Qur'an:

> *"And tell the believing women to reduce some of their vision and guard their private parts and not display their adornment except that which [ordinarily] appears thereof and to draw their headcovers over their chests and not display their adornment [i.e., beauty] except to their husbands, their fathers, their husbands' fathers, their sons, their husbands' sons, their brothers, their brothers' sons, their sisters' sons, their women, that which their right hands possess [i.e., slaves], or those male attendants having no physical desire, or children who are not yet aware of the private aspects of women."*[120]

Additionally:

> *"O Prophet, tell your wives and your daughters and the women of the believers to bring down over themselves [part] of their outer garments.*[121] *That is more suitable that they will be known*[122] *and not be abused. And ever is Allah Forgiving and Merciful."*[123]

Hopefully, one can begin to understand more fully the significance of the *hijab* and realize that it is more than just clothing. It is not, as some mistakenly assume, merely a costume or emblem of Islam. Its purpose is a barrier from

---

[119] There are differing opinions among scholars as to whether or not, to what extent, and under what conditions the face and hands may appear.

[120] *Surah an-Nur,* 24:31.

[121] The *jilbab,* which is defined as a cloak covering the head and reaching to the ground, thereby covering the woman's entire body.

[122] As chaste believing women.

[123] *Surah al-Ahzab,* 33:59.

the opposite sex. Modest behavior is the complement to modest garments, which is encompassed in the Arabic word *"hishmah,"* meaning "modesty, chastity, and decency." The *hijab* is simply a means of protection for the woman when she is out in public. Western women boast about how free and liberated they are, but they are actually driven to wear what men want to see: flesh, legs, arms and breasts. This appears truly to be a form of sexual slavery – submission and servitude to men and their desires.

If Camille Paglia's description of how the male seeks out a female with his "roving eyes" is recalled, it helps to better understand the function of the *hijab* in terms of how it corresponds with basic feminine nature and how it preserves a society from becoming degenerate. Beneath the *hijab* is a woman's body, and its main purpose is to keep her figure and beauty hidden. Whether she is married or not makes no difference. The Muslim woman dresses in a way distinctive from non-Muslim women. In fact, in order for her clothing to be considered *hijab*, it must be purposely different from what unbelieving women wear.[124] The Muslim woman's clothing should be loose and cover all of her body except the face and hands. A woman is not wearing *hijab* if she has on a pair of tight-fitting jeans, leggings or only stockings on her legs. Included in the limitations and guidelines for clothing to be considered Islamic dress is that the fabric must not be sheer or transparent. It should be understood that the Muslim woman dresses this way when she goes out in public or when in front of men who would not be prohibited to her in marriage because of a blood or nursing relationship. When she is in the company of her immediate family members, she may basically wear what she likes.

For those with any honest knowledge of history, the *hijab* is not a new concept. The way religious women

---

[124]*The Islamic Ruling Regarding Women's Dress According to the Quran and Sunnah*, p. 26.

dressed in most ancient civilizations was in a pious, modest fashion, and they veiled. Catholic nuns still wear their habit. Women during the Victorian era wore long dresses with high collars. In the Americas much the same theme continued as the pioneer women wore the same type of long dresses and bonnets. Women during the Victorian age were more respected than women of today. They were esteemed for being chaste and modest, and they certainly were not publicly ostracized for being such. How society's norms have changed for the worse is more than clear.

## The Hijab Fits Women's Nature

The human desire to cover nakedness is a natural impulse. The newborn baby who was safe and warm inside the womb wants nothing more than to be swaddled and kept warm upon birth. The first thing Adam and Eve did upon being chastised by Allah in the Garden was to cover themselves. Even in the liberalized Western society, there are medical texts referring to "exhibitionism" or the practice of showing off the body to strangers as an abnormal disorder which is not compatible with the normal human personality. Is it not possible to correlate the prevalence of exhibitionism or blatant immodesty to the prevalence of sexually violent crimes like harassment and rape? Can it not be agreed that the way women behave and dress has a direct impact on men, both at the workplace and in public, as to how they are treated and valued?

Feminists address the problems of sexual harassment and rape as a male problem rather than a female problem. Legally, rape has always been considered and labeled a violent crime rather than solely a sexually motivated crime. Now, with the advent of date and acquaintance rape, one wonders about the true motivating factor behind all rape. In other words, what is the difference between rape by acquaintances or by strangers? Both situations amount to rape. The Federal Bureau of Investigation defines rape as "attempted or completed vaginal intercourse with a female, forcibly and against her will." What is unusual is that if the rape takes place on federal property, then the federal law applies, but if it occurs on state property, then state law presides. "Both federal and state rape laws have been reformed since the 1970s and are more contemporary than the FBI definition in that they: (a) are gender neutral, meaning either men or women can be victims of rape; (b) cover anal and oral penetration as well as vaginal intercourse and include insertion of objects other than the penis; and (c) extend to non-forcible assaults if intercourse is obtained with someone unable to consent because of mental illness, mental retardation, or intoxication."[125] Sociologists have formed different words for different types of rape. There are now several kinds: stranger rape, acquaintance rape, date rape, and marital rape. The perpetrator of an acquaintance rape is someone who knows something about the victim they assault. Date rape is a specific type of acquaintance that involves a victim and a rapist who already have a level of intimacy with one another. The level of intimacy is not defined, but it can be assumed that they have seen each other voluntarily more than one time.[126] As defined, date rape is when the perpetrator is a friend or boyfriend. But as more stories come forward, it seems clear that there are discrepancies. Date rape appears to be a much more sexually motivated act rather than a violent one. So how does this new twist effect one's thinking about rape in general? Could it be that rape is a combination of sex and violence? Why are women's friends feeling so free to sexually violate them?

---

[125] Mary P. Koss and Sarah Cook, "Facing the Facts – Date and Acquaintance Rape are Significant Problems for Women," *Current Controversies on Family Violence,* Richard Gelles and Donileen Loseke, Sage, 1993, pp. 104-105.
[126] Ibid., p. 105.

And what messages are women sending men by their body language and attitudes?

Although rape has occurred since the beginning of time, today the Western public's awareness to the alarmingly high incidence of rape occurring on the streets and on college campuses is a symptom of a major structural problem of society. As sexual morality and religious values have diminished and been replaced by liberal sexual freedom, the repercussions are finally being felt.

Most women agree that men should control themselves; however, are women not asking too much when they assume they can dress in less clothing and yet blame men for the harassment that occurs as a response? It is interesting that working women know that what they wear has a direct impact on how they are valued and treated in the workplace. Dressing for success has become a de rigeur aspect of a woman's strategy in the ever-competitive workplace. Low-heeled shoes, high-necked blouses, business blazers and longish skirts with a minimum of jewelry is the fashion recipe for many professional women. Yet, these same women may ignore this knowledge and dress quite differently when the working day is done.

Men in Western society are not unhappy with scantily dressed women running about. But women are now trying to get rid of any personal responsibility for their actions. This is contrary to what comes naturally with being a woman. Women must be more in control of their bodies simply because they are the ones subject to being harassed, assaulted, raped or impregnated. Therefore, a dangerous trend can be seen in Western cultures when women expect men to be in control while they want to be free of any responsibility. Contemporary media messages tell women to be offended when a rape victim is asked what she was wearing or doing prior to the rape (as if this had nothing to do with the possible motivation).

Statistics show that date rape is growing by epidemic proportions. It has been estimated that one out of four women will be raped in her lifetime. But when it happens, will they be considered true victims of rape? Or can the social structure be held partially at fault?

As women evolve, a great change in moral standards can be seen. Women were traditionally brought up to be much more responsible. In the 1950s, for example, there were the "good girls" and the "bad girls." This is indeed a different era. One wonders just how far people will go in passing the buck of personal responsibility. By the 1980s women claimed the same right as men to sexual activity without being stigmatized on the basis of being consenting adults. This has now become a determining factor between right and wrong.

## The Islamic Culture

Although it is at times difficult to accept a different way of life and set of values, it is possible. Basically, people have a tendency to accept their given society, its culture and value system without much thought. Therefore, people tend to be conformists and not individualists. Most Westerners do not consider themselves to be conformists and would rather think of themselves as free thinkers. But many of their actions and prejudices reveal otherwise. They are quick to reject other ideas and ways of life before they know the facts. This has been aptly labeled by sociologists as egocentric or xenophobic. In order to grasp different schools of thought, one must therefore reject the idea of being an approval seeker.

To discuss present-day Islamic culture, one could look to Saudi Arabia – a nation striving to implement Islamic law within its society. Saudi Arabia enjoys one of the world's lowest crime rates. More specifically, crimes against women, such as murder, serial killing, sexual harassment and rape, are very rare. Contrary to this, these crimes are a daily occurrence in every major city in Western cultures. Naturally, it cannot be contended that the *hijab* is the sole factor that prevents these crimes, but it does play a major role in developing a setting where both sexes are reminded that men and women should behave themselves accordingly.

In hopes of combating sexual harassment, legislation was employed in the West in the 1960s when more and more women were entering the work force. Incidentally, this legislation did not put a stop to sexual harassment at all. In fact, it helps to confirm suspicions that mere legal sanctions are not enough to deter crimes. Other factors must be reshaped as well. Perhaps punishments were not strict enough, or perhaps there is an urgent need for total social reform. What is evident is that the combination of covered, modest women, strict *shari'ah* laws, and a segregated society deters crimes against women dramatically in Islamic countries. *Shari'ah* jurisprudence has an effective way of deterring rapists, murderers and drug traffickers – they are executed. *Shari'ah* laws and punishments for crimes against women are strict, not lenient. Women and children are highly protected members of society. Certainly, in a true Islamic setting Muslim women are not overridden by worries about their children being abducted or molested.

The way in which women tend to their needs in public and through business can have a great impact on the society and what becomes the "norm." The true Islamic society would not have any sense of a "man's world" or "paradise for men," due largely to how the women appear and behave in public. When women believe in and demonstrate chastity and modesty in both public or private life, it makes Islamic culture a "paradise for women," where they are freed from the oppression Western women face on a daily basis. Muslim women do not feel obligated to serve the desires of men. They are freed from the notion that their role in life is to appear as sex kittens or playthings. When women follow Islam's guidance, the reward is not only in the Hereafter but here on earth because their actions grant them their true dignity as women and as human beings. Islamic wisdom tells that it is women who can change, strengthen or weaken social structure by their will and actions.

Someone once asked columnist Marilyn Vos Savant: "We are taught that the mind and soul are the source of meaning in life. So why are appearances so important to women?" She replied, "If you're referring to how much time women spend on their looks, maybe you've got it backwards. If appearances were so important to women, it would be the men who would be spending all that time."[127] This might explain why unmarried women primp and preen before going out in public, but it creates confusion in terms of why many married women also do the same.

While married women are known for their casual appearances at home, barely spending any time to look pretty for their husbands, they are keen on applying full makeup, doing their hair and dressing up when going outside. Islam encourages the opposite. When going out in public, observant Muslim women cover their faces if they should have on makeup. When they are at home, they are known to dress up and spend quality time looking nice for their husbands. After all, it is them they love and want to be attractive for.

It is assumed that most married women who dress up when they go out are not doing so necessarily to attract men, but it is most probably due to their deeply imbedded belief that they are valued according to how attractive they look. How can women declare they are liberated while being approval seekers who need attention and affirmation? Rather than doing beneficial things to enhance their self-

---

[127]"Ask Marilyn," *Parade Magazine,* July 15, 1994, p. 15.

esteem, they are obsessed with looking beautiful, youthful, and sexy. Since self-esteem is related only to appearance in this instance, one can understand women like Marilyn Monroe who became sex symbols. The Prophet of Islam (ﷺ) foretold this when he said:

> *"There are two types of the inmates of Hell whom I have not seen in my time: people having whips with them like the tails of oxen with which they will beat people and women who are dressed but appear naked who incline to evil and make others incline towards it. Their hair is like the humps of the bukht camel, inclined to one side. They will not enter Paradise, nor will they smell its odor, although its odor can be found from long distances."*[128]

---

[128] Related by Muslim.

# The Segregated Society

## Casual Relations Lead to Casualties

Through casual intermingling of the sexes Western people have lost their personal privacy. They no longer know what personal privacy is. How can a person respect another's privacy when he does not respect his own? Talk shows are aired daily exploiting the most personal aspects of people's lives. They have become stages for moral decay, public humiliation, and a show of the most bizarre and decadent. In Western societies it is not uncommon to meet a perfect stranger and practically hear his life story within five minutes.

In the truly Islamic society Muslim men would be careful to avoid bumping into women in shops. In restaurants, families sit in sections sometimes surrounded by a screen in order to create a private atmosphere. And if a family is sitting together on a picnic, another family would not park too close to them. The true Islamic society fosters a peaceful and unobtrusive social setting. In fact, many non-Muslim family members of pilots who served Saudia Airlines for ten or more years said they enjoyed being exposed to a different way of life and that their experience was rewarding.

In contrast, women in the West may be harassed in public by men whistling or making sexual innuendoes. They are sometimes approached by strange men who want to make small talk or ask them on a date. In an Islamic society these things would not happen. Because a Muslim woman is totally dressed and her figure is not exposed, she has every right to take offense at a man who stares at her, for she is clearly not asking for attention. A woman who is dressing otherwise does not have this privilege.

A survey of 7,000 college students on 32 different campuses showed that one out of four women had been sexually assaulted.[129] In a study by Gordon and Riger a third of females questioned in urban areas throughout the United States said that they were fearful of being raped during certain times and in certain situations. Due to this fear, 50% of the women said they tended to keep away from these activities where they felt vulnerable. When they went outdoors, 51% preferred to be accompanied by other people. In contrast, only 4% of men felt they needed to take such precautions and did not perceive themselves as vulnerable when going out alone.[130] Of the males studied 90% said they did not make any changes in lifestyle as a reaction to any threat they felt in regard to crime or assault: sexual or otherwise. And these men lived in the same neighborhoods as did the females.[131] Since the time these studies were carried out, the system has not changed. In fact, nothing has changed. Women themselves have had to pattern their lives in a paranoid and reclusive way in order to be safe. These statistics tell that American women put up a false front about their sense of security, as it is obvious that they live under the threat of being assaulted. Conversely, men do not share these same fears. From this, inequality between the sexes in America becomes ever more clear, yet few changes are being made to prevent such flagrant abuse of women. While the West prides itself on the integration of the sexes, its failure is evident from the number of casualties who fall by the wayside as statistics.

---

[129]The Strategic Study Group on the Status of Women, Report to the President and the Commission for Women, Recommendation Package #4, Dec. 1987, The Pennsylvania State University, *Sexual Violence Against Women – General Recommendation P,* p. 42.

[130]Mary P. Koss and Sarah Cook, "Facing the Facts – Date and Acquaintance Rape are Significant Problems for Women," *Current Controversies on Family Violence,* Richard Gelles and Donileen Loseke, Sage, 1993, p. 112.

[131]Ibid.

For this very reason it can be better understood why Islam has made men the protectors of women – women are more vulnerable than men. This is precisely why in an Islamic society men and women do not intermingle freely and casually. Furthermore, if a man merely stares at a woman in such a way to annoy her, it is considered harassment and an encroachment of her privacy. And contrary to what some people believe, Muslim women are not prohibited from leaving their homes. They may go out to fulfill their needs.

The regulated Islamic society is more realistic toward the physical differences between men and women. It keeps relations distant, not promoting the laxity or moral degradation which is a natural response to desensitization. In what way is this oppressive for a woman? It is but a safeguard, which in all honesty, is something that makes the Islamic society beautiful to reside in.

## Education for Women and Men

In terms of education Islam upholds the quest for knowledge as vital for both women and men. The Prophet (ﷺ) said:

> "Seeking knowledge is an obligation upon every Muslim."[132]

Although Islam and feminists uphold some of the same principles in regard to women being educated, the feminist demand for equality in terms of sameness creates a wide division between the two because Islam calls for the protection of women. There was a time in Western culture when women were protected by the male members of their families. They were escorted in public and chaperoned on dates. They certainly were not left alone with men if they

---

[132] Related by at-Tabarani – *saheeh*.

were not married. Their fathers took a greater role in guiding and protecting them and in finding them suitable men to marry. What happened? It seems the "liberation" of women also changed men and made them feel less protective of them.

Higher education for American women was not stressed prior to the 1960s and the Women's Liberation Movement. It was only legally required for girls to be educated to the eighth grade and for boys to the twelfth. At that time there were very few institutions of higher education that would accept women. As things progressed there was a small surge in the number of all girls' schools. However, that was short lived, and as social norms shaped morality, nearly all of these schools were replaced by coed facilities. If this has not created enough troubles, other areas clearly point to the inequality between men and women even upon graduating with the same degree.

A television documentary in 1992 explored medical students, both male and female, who, as they neared graduation, were finding their futures bleak. Upon graduation many realized that with the extra burden of paying back thousands of dollars for their education in the form of interest-bearing loans, they would be living just near the poverty level for the first ten years of practice. For women this meant it was time to rethink their career and educational choices, but not so for the male student. The female student figured that after ten years of practice she would be in her mid-thirties. By that time she might have to stop working in order to begin a family. Such thought processes and burdens are for women only.

## **The Coed Facility and Man's Paradise**

In Western cultures nearly all public schools, including college campuses, are coed. In recent years dormitories and student housing facilities have become integrated as well. In the beginning of coeducational settings many parents were worried and did not like the idea, but as time passed, desensitization set in and they came to accept it. However, the trend persists and so do college drinking parties, teen pregnancy, and cases of venereal disease. Henry Wechsler, director of the Alcohol Studies Program at Harvard School of Public Health, said his team surveyed 17,592 students on 140 U.S. campuses in 1993. The results were listed in the Journal of the American Medical Association as follows: "Forty-four percent reported binging[133] on alcohol on at least one occasion in the two weeks before the survey. At about one third of the schools more than 50% of the students were bingers." A problem defined in the study was "that nearly half of U.S. college students who are given to alcohol make life miserable for much of the other half." The study further cited, "At big drinking schools sober students were twice as likely as those at the lower-level schools to be insulted or humiliated; to be pushed, hit or assaulted; and to experience unwanted sexual advances."[134]

The aforementioned liberal practice of coeducational facilities is in direct contrast to what would be described as an Islamic education, where all levels of education are segregated, except, perhaps, the very first grades of elementary school and kindergarten. This sets a very different stage for learning in comparison to the West's education system, where school is equated with a place to practice social interaction. Education structured Islamically is not necessarily thought of as a place of social importance. It is more conducive to learning and is less distracting for both genders. The student's attention is on learning rather

---

[133]Defined as downing five drinks in a row for men and four in a row for women.
[134]Study by Henry Wechsler, "Collegians' Drunkenness Ruining Campus Life for Many Sober Students," *Arab News,* 1993.

than sexual thought processes. This is very helpful during the teen years when hormones begin to change. In Islamic settings Muslim families do not have the various life-altering and sometimes life-threatening problems experienced in Western cultures, such as teen delinquency, drug and alcohol abuse, rape, or teen pregnancy.

One dean, who has been working on college campuses for twenty-five years, expressed that physical and sexual abuse towards women "has been occurring all along." And he voiced his opinion, "Now, the problem is out of the closet, thank goodness... society isn't going to tolerate sexual abuse as appropriate behavior anymore. The whole consciousness has changed. Everyone views the body as private."[135] If he is referring to Western trends, then he is sadly mistaken. With only a quick glance into the public, the magazine stands, the television and video markets, the way men and women interact with one another, and the way women show off their bodies in public, there is no indication to the validity of his statement. The Western woman's body is not kept private whatsoever. The fact is, she is exposing more and more than ever before.

The problems created by coed facilities do not only plague college students. Problems begin at earlier ages, in the junior high and high school levels, where students face invasion of their privacy due to a poorly fashioned education system. Surveys are making some startling revelations. One article devoted pages to outline what parents of the 1990s are facing. It included this alarming statistic: "It is projected that 40% of American 14-year old girls will get pregnant by the time they are 19 years old."[136] As the evidence mounts,

---

[135]*The Record,* "Sexual Abuse on Campus, Where is the True Gentlemen Today?" Center for Women Studies, The Pennsylvania State University, Spring, 1987, p. 7.

[136]Hal Mattern, "Good Values vs. Bad Influences," *The Arizona Republic,* Section H, September 5, 1993.

casual relations between the sexes has created numerous problems which must be addressed. How long will it be before changes are implemented in order to save many women from being victimized?

## Academic Sexual Harassment

Another problem eliminated by the segregation of sexes among both students and faculty in an Islamic school is that called "academic sexual harassment." Academic sexual harassment is "the use of authority to emphasize the sexuality or sexual identity of a student in a manner which prevents or impairs the student's full enjoyment of educational benefits, climate or opportunities."[137] It can be gathered from this definition that the victim defines whether or not a comment or action constitutes academic sexual harassment. If the victim is not threatened or does not feel coerced, then the act is not an offense. So to one student a professor's comments or actions might not seem threatening but to another the same might be felt and labeled harassment.

The team of Benson and Thomson took a random number of female students. Their sample was comprised of 269 women who were students entering their senior year at the Berkeley campus. Their study showed that 59% of women said sexual harassment happens occasionally, and one third or more said they knew a victim of sexual harassment. Additionally, 29.7% of the women said they had been sexually harassed from their male professors while at college.[138]

Another study done by Lott, Reilly and Howard took a survey sample of 927 women and men. They were either

---

[137] Linda Rubin and Sherry Borgers, "Sexual Harassment in Universities During the 1980s," *Sexual Harassment – Confrontations and Decisions,* pp. 49-50.
[138] Ibid., p. 29.

students, faculty, or other staff from the University of Rhode Island. Thirteen percent of these people said they knew someone who had been sexually harassed. "Personal knowledge of the sexual intimidation of another person was reported in 68 cases (7.3%)."[139]

Wilson and Kraus performed an investigation into sexual harassment of both undergraduate and graduate students at East Carolina University. Of the 108 men and 226 women, 33% of the women said they had been sexually assaulted by their male professors. The kinds of assaults were defined as 20.2% verbal harassment, 15.4% staring or looking intently, 13.6% comments about what the woman was wearing, her figure or sexual attitudes, 8.9% unwanted touching, patting or pinching, 4.9% slight coercion for some kind of sexual activity, 2.2% demanded sexual favors, and .9% were physically assaulted.[140]

## A Woman's Right to Peace and Justice

Sexual harassment is a common occurrence in Western society, due, among other things, to the free and unrestrained mixing of the sexes. The manmade system is one which exposes women to continual abuse and harassment. The fact is that a large majority of Western women do not understand what is going on because they have become desensitized. They know no other way. The process of socialization makes reality sometimes difficult to assess. Many naively think things will eventually become better if they stay on course. They want to believe that one day they will be liberated.

Sexual harassment is not new, but it has been occurring more often and in much more obvious ways for at least the past decade. The structure of the society is not the only

---

[139]Ibid., p. 29.
[140]Ibid., p. 29.

reason. When dealing with men and women who are sexually liberated, who have no set standard of morality and no base of religion, it is no wonder that men feel free to approach or assault women at random. Men and women in Western society have grown far too familiar with one another, and this sets the stage for men to freely violate and invade a woman's privacy.

Recent sexual harassment cases such as those of Paula Jones and Anita Hill have helped to denounce this horrendous, flagrant offense against the working woman in hopes of helping more women understand that sexual harassment need not be tolerated. Recently in 1995, Mr. Packwood, an American senator, was forced to resign because he was accused of several accounts of alleged sexual harassment, sexual assault and other sexual indecencies. As these cases go public, women are being reminded that sexual harassment can happen anywhere and happens more often in places of business once designated as male-only territory. Yet, even though these cases have been exploited in the media, the truth is that if a woman is being sexually harassed in the workplace, she is still hesitant to punish her harasser. So women endure it and have even grown to accept it because they cannot risk losing their jobs. Added to this fear is the problem of taking an offender to court; it is a lengthy, costly process. In addition, it is not always so easy to prove sexual harassment, as it can be accomplished in many ways when no one else is around to witness it.

It is apparent that sexual harassment becomes a more common and serious problem when women work with men who are in superior positions over them. What surprises everyone is that even if women are not in subordinate positions, they, too, are being assaulted and harassed. According to the U.S. 9th Circuit Court of Appeals, things are not looking good even for higher level professional women, for "60% of women lawyers practicing in federal courts in nine western states, including Arizona, have experienced sexual harassment."[141] Furthermore, "A third of female attorneys said a male colleague had harassed them in the past five years, 40% said a client had harassed them, and 6% said they had been harassed by a judge."[142] In a study of sexual harassment on the college campus of Berkeley in 1994, out of 269 women in the study group, 59% said they had "occasionally" experienced it, and 29.7% had been sexually harassed by their male college professors.[143]

A popular saying in the West asserts there is no harm in "mixing business with pleasure." In realistic terms, however, sexual harassment should include any and all invasions of a woman's privacy. In an Islamic environment when men and women must work together, women wear *hijab,* and interaction is kept within the bounds of professional decency.

Following Islamic guidance protects women to the degree that no man other than her husband or close male relatives is entitled to even touch her hand. The common, casual handshake is not proper for Muslim men and women to practice. The more one learns about Islam, the clearer it becomes that every aspect of life is addressed. Every ordinance is perfect, and there are no contradictions. The guidance is clear and precise, and there is a reason of goodness behind each one. Where societies based on other systems have failed in granting a woman peace and justice, Islam has produced one in her favor.

---

[141]*Arizona Republic,* Los Angeles Times, Santa Barbara California: "60% of Women Lawyers in 9 States Report Sexual Harassment in Study," A3, August 23, 1993.
[142]Ibid.
[143]Linda Rubin and Sherry Borgers, "Sexual Harassment in Universities During the 1980s," *Sexual Harassment – Confrontations and Decisions,* p. 29.

# Moral Liberation of the Western Woman

During the Women's Liberation Movement of the 1960s and 70s, the word "liberated" lost much of its authentic meaning. It ended up meaning morally free. Women mistakenly thought being liberated meant freedom from traditional moral guidelines and virtuous lifestyles.

The 1960s was a hectic decade. It was a time of upheaval and unrest. Not only was the Vietnam War being waged, but the assassination of President Kennedy shook the American public's emotional stability. Anti-war demonstrations were sparked, not necessarily because Americans did not believe in the war, but because the media had penetrated the war zone and revealed how illegal, inhumane, and bloody Vietnam really was. Footage of bombed civilian villages was splashed across the television. Bloodied Vietnamese women lay on the ground as toddlers stared teary-eyed at their mother's lifeless body. A popular slogan summed up what most of the public thought of these barbaric scenes: "Make love, not war." Peace messages flooded the airways and streets. Hippies (or "flower children") sent signals to the public and Washington to stop the war.

Coincidentally, this is when the new interpretations of liberation made their entrance. Women's voices began to chant the most popular words of the era: freedom, peace, love and liberation. The birth control pill was marketed. This was among the causes of the sexual revolution. Experimentation was the byword – and the more, the better. Women's lives were irrevocably altered. Relations between the sexes deteriorated further. Couples began living together comfortably outside of marriage, and fashion was exposing more of women's bodies.

As mentioned earlier, men and women experience life in fundamentally different ways due to their physical and emotional makeup. These differences are highlighted once a man and woman begin a relationship, whether inside or outside of marriage. Allan Bloom, professor and author, summed up the physical differences of men and women: "Man in a state of nature, either in the first one or the one we have now, can walk away from a sexual encounter and never give it another thought. But a woman may have a child, and in fact, as becomes ever clearer, may want to have a child. Sex can be an indifferent thing for men, but it really cannot quite be so for women. This is what might be called the female drama. Modernity promised that all human beings would be treated equally. Women took that promise seriously and rebelled against the old order. But as they have succeeded, men have also been liberated from their old constraints. And women, now liberated and with equal careers, nevertheless find they still have a desire to have children but have no basis for claiming that men should share their desire for children or assume a responsibility for them. So nature weighs more heavily on women."[144] Professor Bloom admits that men can be very callous about free sex (premarital or extramarital).

Islam's stance on sexual relations between a man and woman who are not married is that it is strictly sanctioned and punished, whether the offenders are married to other individuals or if they are single. The Arabic term is *zina*. *Zina* is considered morally wrong and a major sin:

> *"And do not approach unlawful sexual intercourse.*[145] *Indeed, it is ever an immorality and is evil as a way."*[146]

---

[144]*The Closing of the American Mind*, p. 114.
[145]i.e., avoid all situations that might possibly lead to it.
[146]*Surah al-Isra'*, 17:32.

The Prophet (ﷺ) said that *zina* is the greatest sin following *shirk* (association of something with Allah). And he (ﷺ) said:

> *"There is no sin after shirk greater in the eyes of Allah than a drop of semen which a man places in the womb which is not lawful for him."*[147]

As previously stated, Islam prohibits both fornication and adultery and applies strict punishment upon those found guilty. For this reason Muslims steer clear from even the paths that might lead to a relationship. The punishment for *zina* for unmarried persons is one hundred lashes and exile for one year. For married adulterers it is stoning to death. The reason *zina* is so strictly sanctioned is because Islam holds foremost the sanctity of life, family and marriage (as the legal means through which people engage in sexual relations and bring children into the world). Therefore, Islam makes no apologies for its strict retribution for those who openly commit *zina*. However, in order for a person to be punished for *zina*, the following must be ascertained concerning the offender: 1) mental competence, 2) puberty, 3) willing participation, 4) knowledge of the divine prohibition, and 5) confession of the act or the testimony of four witnesses that they actually saw the act take place, which is not easy to obtain unless the parties are flaunting the practice publicly.

Without deterrent punishments, illicit sex would run rampant as it has in the West. Again, Islam firmly protects the family structure with consistent laws which combine belief with action. In the Western culture a conglomerate of choices and freedoms exist. The benefit of a strong family unit is verbalized, but personal actions, social structure, norms and laws do not make it a reality. Islam proudly maintains that there is no substitute for the family unit and

---

[147] Reported by al-Bukhari.

that marriage is the legal means for sexual relations. Islam protects the family unit and does not consider having children out of wedlock an acceptable "mistake." In the West the sanction against extramarital affairs has been drastically reduced by the "no fault divorce" laws, whereby there is no longer a stigma or penalty in divorce for having committed adultery. Sexual relations outside of marriage by unmarried people (fornication) are not even considered unlawful in the West. It is simply considered a way of life. Often times, premarital sex is considered a problem only when an unwanted pregnancy occurs. This is especially true for underage minors because then it becomes the family's problem.

Following such moral decline and liberalization, a whole host of other problems have fed off one another. Marriage has become obsolete – no one feels they have to get married because one can be sexually fulfilled without it. Sexually transmitted diseases have spread. Children are born out of wedlock or else abortion is resorted to. The Western man is altogether free from constraint by both legal and moral means. He is free to be irresponsible and untrustworthy. Therefore, the claims of theorists, professors and sociologists that the family unit is still strong and viable today can be rejected. The stability of the family has all but disintegrated, as the manmade system has neglected it.

Premarital and extramarital sex have destroyed relations between the sexes and threaten the stability of the family everyday in the West. Yet, hypocritically, most of Western society "righteously" condemns the legal practice of polygamy, which is the lawful right of a Muslim man to have more than one wife. Polygamy may sound strange, but it exists, everywhere; perhaps not in its fullest sense (as a man having more than one legal wife) but certainly as a man having or desiring another woman. Historically, men have proven in their private lives (and today in public) that they have the tendency to want more than one woman. Their willingness to venture outside the norms and even legal laws says something about their true nature.

In reality, polygamy today is rarely spoken about, accepted by people, or practiced according to the *sunnah* (prophetic way). Polygamy should not be practiced in any other way, and it is not a prescription for an already bad marriage, as some falsely assert. By far, the biggest threat to polygamy is the attitudes women have towards the men they love: possessiveness, ownership and jealousy.

It has been well documented that the plurality of wives can work, even within the same home: all living together, maturely, and as partners. Numerous non-Muslim philosophers, both ancient and modern, students of science and therapists have found beyond a doubt the true seed of polygamy implanted in man by his Creator. In his book *Sexuality,* Jeffrey Weeks says the major differences between men and women rests in how men are naturally more inclined towards competition, polygamy, and feelings of jealousy, while females are generally more "malleable" by nature and are prone to be more agreeable.[148]

Arthur Schopenhauer, a German philosopher (1788-1860), said in his writing *Supplements to the World as Will and Idea,* "There is no arguing about polygamy; it must be taken as *de facto* existing everywhere, and the only question is how it shall be regulated. We all live, at any rate for a time, and most of us always in polygamy. And so, since every man needs many women, there is nothing fairer than to allow him, nay, to make it incumbent upon him, to provide for many women."[149]

In Islam the husband is totally financially responsible for his wives and children. He is legally bound to provide

---

[148] *Sexuality,* p. 49.
[149] *The Great Thoughts,* p. 412.

for each wife on an equal basis and cannot play favor to one while neglecting another:

> *"And you will never be able to be equal [in feeling] between wives, even if you should strive [to do so]. So do not incline completely [toward one] and leave another hanging."*[150]

If he chooses to marry another wife, he must take into consideration the additional cost to clothe, feed, and house her and their possible future children. Western men condone their own irresponsible illicit affairs with women and prostitutes but condemn the more responsible, humane allowance of polygamy. Islamic guidance prohibits the selfish desires of men and makes them responsible people.

Reasons for having more than one wife have been described in a variety of ways. One might be that the first wife is unable to bear children. Instead of callously divorcing her, the husband marries another woman in order to have children. Another reason for having a second wife is when there is a health problem related to sexual dysfunction which, if not resolved, causes a strain on the marriage. It is possible, as well, that the man could feel a need for more sex than the wife is able to easily give. In societies where women greatly outnumber men, polygamy helps provide for women who would otherwise remain unmarried.

If a Muslim woman feels strongly against her husband having another wife, she may request a divorce. But it is important to remember that while Muslim men may marry up to four wives, they must also be able to take on the great responsibility. Men are given this warning in the Qur'an:

> *"...Then marry those that please you of [other] women, two or three or four. But if you fear that you will not be just, then [marry only] one..."*[151]

---

[150] *Surah an-Nisa'*, 4:129.
[151] *Surah an-Nisa'*, 4:3.

In the end, the reasons to marry more than one wife vary according to personal conviction, but no one can prevent a Muslim man from doing so.

Without a doubt this discussion is sure to have raised red warning flags in some readers' minds. One might be, "Why can a Muslim man have more than one wife, while the woman is allowed only one husband?" Firstly, women, in general, do not have the innate tendency or desire. Secondly, if a woman had more than one husband, how would the paternity of children be determined? Although blood tests can sometimes determine this, they cannot determine it until after the birth. Thirdly, what would happen if one of the husbands died thereby leaving her with the other husband and all the children? It would not be fair to make a man financially, legally and emotionally responsible for someone else's children. And medically, it is more threatening for a woman to have multiple sexual partners. Additionally, what would happen to a woman with two husbands if she became pregnant? How would this effect the husband who is not presumed to be the father of the unborn child in terms of wanting sexual relations with his already pregnant wife? Although women are usually able to continue sexual relations throughout pregnancy, would it not be a burden if she had more than one husband to fulfill? To carry the supposition further, how would the father of the unborn child feel about the other man should something happen as a result of him having sex with the woman during her pregnancy, such as premature delivery or miscarriage?

Hopefully, there is now a better understanding of polygamy as regards its practice, sanctions, permissibility and restrictions. According to the Qur'an, polygamy is lawful for all men. Therefore, Muslim women and men accept polygamy, as it is a permission granted by Allah for the benefit and given circumstances of differing societies of all times.

To close the topic of morality in the West, the willingness of women to give themselves to men outside of marriage is degrading. Premarital sex is the greatest, self-inflicted devaluation of the human. According to Islam, an individual's actions cannot be considered a right if it negatively impacts society as a whole. The Western mind has become so self-centered that the safety and well-being of society is totally absent from one's thinking. The forces of the Women's Liberation Movement promoted the idea that the human body is something to be proud of, to show, and to share with whomever. While doing so, women chanted themes of self-actualization, self-fulfillment, recognition and equality. But were the ensuing consequences worth it?

## Redefining Abortion

Although birth control pills help women be sexually liberated, are easily available and not too costly, it is apparent that there are still many women who do not use them. Current statistics estimate that 4 million women seek abortions each year in the United States.[152] Some legal clinics upholding the right to abortion call themselves clever names to reduce the guilt associated with abortion, like "Family Planning Services" and "Planned Parenthood." Women advocates asked Congress to pass a bill that would cover the costs for unlimited abortions under Medicare. They explained to Congress and the public that these are unwanted pregnancies that women should be entitled to terminate. "It is the woman's body and life we are dealing with, and she should be free to do with her body as she chooses in regards to the life within her."[153]

If this amounts to the termination of healthy, viable human life, then why don't they call it murder? What these

---

[152]Televised court hearing of the U.S. Senate Congress, August 2, 1994.
[153]Ibid.

feminists are attempting to ensure is their right to do anything with themselves, regardless of anyone else. But what about the impact this liberalization has on society? Their thinking is erroneous. We do not create ourselves. Life is a gift that develops in the womb, and when left unencumbered, proceeds in due course upon its own volition. It is obvious that these women do not believe in the sanctity of life. Only God gives and takes life, and He said, "Thou shall not kill."

Feminist views on life in the womb have determined that the heartbeat indicates the presence of life, and they have conveniently rejected most medical opinions that life begins at conception. Very soon after conception the formation of the heart takes shape under the chin of the very young embryo, which if left alone, will one day beat. Apparently, life is as cheap as their sentiments and can be flushed away for a fee.[154] Today, abortions performed without any medical explanation or reason are nothing more than a means of birth control for the millions of women who have a "problem" and want a fast solution. For those who are skeptical about the flagrant abuse of abortion in America, the Alan Guttmacher Institute (a Planned Parenthood research division) performed a recent sample survey of 1,900 women who had abortions. The findings are startlingly: 3% of abortions were performed due to implications which threatened the mother's health, another 3% when something was wrong with the baby, and only 1% were done as a response to rape or incest. This leaves a whopping 93%, 16% of which were done because the mother was not sure how the baby would change her life; 21% were not prepared for the responsibility; another 21% said they could not afford the baby; 12% mentioned that their relationship was not

---

[154]In 1995, the woman of the famous Roe vs. Wade decision (which legalized abortion during the first trimester of pregnancy over thirty years ago) changed her views after a religious conversion.

cohesive enough or an absent father; 11% said they just were not responsible or old enough; and 8% said they had enough children and simply did not want the child.[155]

Are these viable reasons to snuff out a life? Even for the most liberal-minded people this has to be a bit shocking. The legalization and access to unlimited abortions have paved the way to the removal of the necessary human component of responsibility between men and women who are having sexual relations. Western society has accepted this as reasonable and rational.

Our Creator exhorts mankind to respect the sanctity of all life:

**"And do not kill yourselves [or one another]. Indeed, Allah is to you ever Merciful."**[156]

Therefore, Islam forbids abortion and considers it a murderous crime. However, if it is medically proven that the pregnancy is going to harm the woman, then abortion is allowed. Islamic guidance is the surest way to human dignity and the preservation of life.

## Vocations for Women

Contrary to what has been said by some, Islam allows women to work outside the home. In fact, Prophet Muhammad's wife, Khadijah, was herself an accomplished business woman. She was a merchant who owned and managed her own prosperous venture. Nonetheless, the image most appealing to the Western imagination is that of the elusive, veiled woman who lives in subjection and fear of her authoritative husband. Westerners think that because a Muslim woman keeps a low profile that she does not have a life! Their imagination conjures up scenes of her being in

---

[155] *The Way Things Ought to Be*, p. 52.
[156] *Surah an-Nisa'*, 4:29.

isolation, hidden from others, and reserved only for the husband's view and carnal delight. This is their fantasy but not the truth.

There are, however, certain vocations Muslim women will not enter, such as those in which they are expected to be in the private company of a man or those in which they must expose their bodies. Apart from these, all other professions are lawful for Muslim women providing the work is not demeaning and allows them to adhere to Islamic principles with respect to dress and modest behavior. In contrast, women in the West have been led to believe that working as a man's private secretary, for example, is acceptable and not harmful or demeaning. A woman may take such a job out of necessity, and there is typically no stigma attached to it in her society. However, Western women often complain among themselves about their male bosses and the sexual harassment or abuse they endure.

The art world has always preferred the woman's body. She is everywhere – photographs, movies, magazines, television commercials, billboards and the fashion runways. Sex sells, and her beauty is being used for it. For women the jobs are lucrative. Professional models make millions to show off their bodies but are expected to wear demeaning accessories like pink, cotton candy hair, black makeup, and dog chains or leashes around their necks. They concede in order to keep their popular standing in the fashion industry. The model may be projected as a sensual, sexy plaything one minute or a slithering, amicable creature the next. Suzy Menkes of the international Herald Tribune took a poke at current modeling trends, criticizing, "The revolutionary idea is that models should go back to showing off clothes instead of their bodies."[157]

---

[157] Verena Niemeyer, "Supermodels No Longer Flying," *Arab News,* April 20, 1995.

Fashion designer Calvin Klein had to pull a large campaign ad in 1995 because he was accused of allegedly using under age male and female models. Incidentally, these minors were posed in sexually suggestive postures and wore clothing from the Calvin Klein collection that was provocatively unbuttoned, unzipped, etc. at strategic body points. One wonders where the parents of these child models were, and how, in good conscience, could they consent to seeing their son or daughter so blatantly exploited? Klein was accused of exploitation, but only because children are not considered to have legal consent. So why all the commotion? In such a liberal society, why should age make such a significant difference? From this line of thinking it can be gathered that the only element distinguishing modeling from exploitation is the age of the model. Is nothing considered immoral when people consent? Thus, women posing for *Playboy* are not considered to be exploiting themselves because they are consenting adults. This rational could also explain why there is a growing acceptance of homosexuality in the West. A practice that since the beginning of time has been considered deviant is today under the ever-widening influence of liberalism, no longer considered wrong or immoral.

As Muslim girls reach puberty, they are encouraged to dress modestly. In the West, however, the older girls become the more immodestly they dress in public. Instead of covering their blossoming bodies, they are cued and prompted to show more leg, more cleavage, and more of their navels. What a dichotomy of values!

## **Cosmetic Surgery for the Sake of Approval**

Women, especially models and actresses, are known to be willing patrons of cosmetic surgery. Hollywood is cruel toward the aging process, and the cameras do not lie. There are just so many tricks that photography, lighting, and makeup can do until one must go under the knife. Actresses over the age of forty are the biggest patrons of plastic surgery, dermabrasion, eye lifts, butt lifts, and total reconstructive facial surgery. Age, as Hollywood defines it, is based upon how well a woman appears. If an actress can afford to have a lot of good cosmetic surgery, then her position in Hollywood is kept open.

Such motivation is not reserved for actresses or models alone. Today, the value of looking youthful, perfect and beautiful has transcended from Hollywood and the fashion runway and has been planted deeply into the Western psyche. A woman's appearance is so connected to her sense of self-worth that many are obsessed with their looks. Literally millions of Western women have had silicone breast implants in order to enhance their self-esteem and attention from men. However, they are now paying a high price, as often times the implants leak cancer-causing silicone into the body. The possibility of the implants rupturing from over stimulation interferes with the sexuality of some women. Often times an implant recipient will undergo second and third surgeries to correct swelling problems, infections and other difficulties. "Virtually all silicone implants, including those with their shells intact, 'bleed' silicone into the body," the Food and Drug Administration tells us thirty years too late, after the first implants were made.[158] More alarmingly, the FDA's updates state that 10% of women who had silicone implants received a kind that has a coating of polyurethane foam. This coating commonly breaks down and releases a by-product element called TDA. TDA has been proven to cause cancer in test animals, and more importantly, has been detected in the breast milk of these implant patients. The health threat to the infants who drink the milk is currently unknown.[159]

---

[158] *Women Pay More (and How to Put a Stop to It)*, p. 40.
[159] Ibid., p. 41.

Western culture is saturated with media messages that promote the value of women in terms of their body image, shape, beauty and age. Youthfulness rates high in such a culture. What is interesting is that these same values hardly exist for men. It does not matter how old a man becomes; he is still appreciated and valued for who he is. It is his personality, accomplishments, and moral stance that are looked at and admired. Women, however, are constantly bombarded by media messages that tell them they must fight the aging process. They frequent cosmetic departments looking at all the anti-aging, anti-wrinkling gimmicks in hopes of finding a cure. What they end up with is a small, one ounce jar that is outrageously expensive, the price of which they gladly pay. While medical sciences do not emphasize enough the danger of sun exposure and the importance of a good diet, the cosmetic industry makes a killing off the Western woman's low self-esteem. Beauty, even if fake, temporary, expensive, or a health risk, is the ultimate aim.

This imaging has affected women more deeply than most realize. It has not only lowered the average woman's self-esteem, it has also affected the way women perceive motherhood. When women are valued according to their outer appearance, then pregnancy itself places a great burden on a woman's mental state. She is going to gain weight, and her youthful breasts and hip sizes are going to change too, sometimes leaving her with stretch marks in both areas. Motherhood is definitely not portrayed by the media as a glamorous position either. Numerous television shows, commercials and movie themes impress upon the woman's mind that women who stay home with children become fat and sloppy. It warns women of the time-consuming demands of motherhood and makes women feel they are going to be giving up too much in return for a family. In this way the system tells young women that being a working woman is much more gratifying, so many women are marrying at much older ages and having their first child after thirty.

## From Silicone Implants to Silicone Bottles

Breastfeeding is a topic Western culture has almost dismissed as unnecessary and primitive. But there are some support groups available for women who breastfeed, such as La Leche League. This educational support system instills in women the importance of breastfeeding. It deals with the questions new mothers have about nursing. In Western culture there is an extensive use of artificial milk products for newborn infants. Although doctors and pediatricians worldwide inform mothers that breast milk is the best nutritional source for newborns, the majority of Western women do not even attempt to feed their babies their own breast milk. Instead, they buy formulas and plastic bottles with silicone nipples. Yet, bottle-fed babies make more trips to the doctor than babies who are breastfed.

Another inhibitor of breastfeeding is the way that Western women perceive their bodies. They are afraid that breastfeeding will change the shape of their breasts. But breastfeeding is good for the mother. It has been proven to help the uterus return to normal size faster after giving birth. Current studies are beginning to link breast cancer with women who have never breastfed but who have been pregnant, implying that breastfeeding might be a necessary function after pregnancy. However, many women in the West are given pills within hours after delivery to dry up their breasts.

Naturally, as the role of mother is cast aside as a lesser role and the roles for women are now found outside the home, women are having to gear up for an exchange of stresses. While having small children has been described as a very stressful time for women, now they are free to experience other stresses in exchange.

In contrast, a Muslim woman would not exhibit such feelings towards motherhood or their bodies. According to Islam, real beauty is the character of a woman, not merely her physical appearance or the texture of her skin. Islam teaches women to value themselves more in terms of how they are living up to the standards of their religion. They are taught that their morality and actions are more impressive and important than their physical appearance. Living Islamically instills peace and confidence, which is possibly the best beauty treatment available. Another positive feature of living Islamically is that one's self-esteem blossoms from the knowledge and satisfaction that it is according to the way in which God wants it to be. Islamic living also benefits in other ways. For example, cleanliness is another very important value, and this must be the first rule in relation to beauty. Ablution (cleansing parts of the body with water five times per day) is beneficial for the skin. The month-long yearly fast is acknowledged to be of great physical, spiritual and medical benefit. And the Prophet (ﷺ) also warned against overeating.

The human body, mind and spirit derive numerous benefits from a properly-lived Islamic lifestyle. By God's will, total health and natural beauty are the results of a divinely-ordained lifestyle. While pleasing Allah, the body and soul are also nourished. Who could ask for more?

## Family Needs a Mother

To get a feeling of how the new generation has come to loath the idea or mere mention of motherhood, consider a protesting, angered young woman (perhaps in her early twenties) walking down a crowded sidewalk at Pennsylvania State University. She was heard responding to her male friend who apparently made a cutting remark, "Well, you said I looked like a thirty-year old mother!" (What worse condition could a woman find herself in?) According to this woman and apparently her male counterpart, nothing could be more detestable, more horrifying or more degrading than to be compared to a middle-aged mother. Thirty years of age can hardly be considered old, yet this woman, representative of the new generation, apparently thought she had only ten more "good" years left to live.

In Western culture it is obvious that both men and women are evolving through a process of dehumanization. The system promotes everything but true human dignity and family life. Although the cornerstone of all societies should be the family, this belief no longer firmly exists in the West. To the new generation the myth of motherhood and family life is a process of the past no longer of value. Women now feel that the time they might spend raising a family is a waste of time and a big mistake. The new generation knows the stigmas about women who become wives and mothers and stay home to run a family. They know how vulnerable a woman becomes once she does this. If her marriage fails and she is divorced, she will find the court system does not care about the years she has invested towards her family. She will have to fight and scratch her way to winning any financial support or retribution.

The modern-day thinking that mothers and wives can be replaced is cold and cruel. Wives can be replaced by girlfriends and prostitutes, and mothers can be replaced by social services. It is a great injustice that women in Western cultures are forced by economic need, pop-culture, media, government and even husbands to forfeit motherhood. Feminists especially do not want to hear about women who are devoted to their families. They would much rather talk and fight for women to work outside the home. It would do them well to be reminded that even highly educated career women would like to stop at some point in their lives to begin a family. This part of women's nature has not yet been destroyed altogether.

Because people work so hard at their jobs and careers, numerous social services have been implemented to take the place of family. Instead of family members coming together on their own to solve problems, individuals must go to counseling, group therapy or other social services to seek help, attention, guidance or support. There are literally hundreds of organizations that are replacing the family unit: nurseries and daycare centers, nursing homes, psychiatric wards, domestic abuse hot lines, homes for unwed mothers, women's crisis centers, teen suicide hot lines, adoption centers and homes for the mentally challenged. Although there will always be some who have nowhere else to turn, what about those who have family? The family unit is often times replaced with institutions, telephone numbers, high priced psychiatrists, and contact with strangers who do not really know the afflicted one. All of these services are a sign that the system has exchanged the family for institutionalism.

With all the dehumanization taking place, perhaps people will eventually lose a vital part of the human personality. The human race seems to be on a crash course toward destruction. People living in major American cities are hardened, desensitized and seem more like robots. Man is not just an intelligent animal endowed with a greater reasoning ability, as some philosophers contend. Rather, man is an entirely different species with a personality that has the capacity for compassion, love, humanity, and spirituality. In the Western civilization today all of this is considered emotionalism, romanticism and a foolish quest for bygone times. The West is indeed evolving, but into what? Who wants to substitute real human closeness and love in exchange for a cold, inhumane world?

The issue of the diminishing role of the mother goes to the heart of what divides man from the animal kingdom. Humans are dependent upon the emotional benefits of having family members there for them, whether they are infants, children, teens, or adults. The significance of the mother and a close-knit family is not only an economic problem. It is not only a social problem, and it is not only a feminist problem. It is a personal problem that no building, corporation, institute or psychologist can take the place of. Personal self-sufficiency is good for every person, and giving women the personal freedom to choose a career should be granted them. However, when women are being forced economically or by social norms to leave their newborn in a daycare, it seems not only cruel from the mother's perspective, but is a cruel introduction to life from the baby's point of view.

## Progress and Civilization

The new generation of youth has become lazy in the quest for knowledge, egocentric, and closed-minded. They are self-centered, extremely autonomous, and very independent. Professor Bloom's perception of modern trends and their impact on college kids is further proof of the family's degradation. Bloom spends a great deal of time and effort to explain today's youth. He says, "People sup together, play together, travel together, but they do not think together. Hardly any homes have any intellectual life whatsoever, let alone one that informs the vital interest of life. Educational TV marks the high tide for family intellectual life."[160]

Bloom aptly describes all the invading media messages and other influences of modern life which makes it a battle for conscientious parents. "Along with the constant newness of everything and the ceaseless moving from place to place, first radio, then television, have assaulted and overturned the privacy of the home, the real American privacy, which permitted the development of a higher and more independent

---

[160]*The Closing of the American Mind,* p. 58.

life within democratic society. Parents can no longer control the atmosphere of the home, and have even lost the will to do so."[161] No truer words could be spoken. One hundred years ago parenting was much less stressful, simplified and was not so governmentally controlled. There was no television, little mass communication, fewer mixed messages, and more family solidarity. Today, the scenario is much different. Homes are bombarded daily with the internet and television that contain visuals and storylines that are either sexually explicit or violent. According to Islam, much of the content of these so-called forms of entertainment can be classified as pornographic. The educational system has invaded the privacy of the home by taking liberties to teach morality. Instead of teaching abstinence in sex education courses or during discussions on AIDS or sexually transmitted diseases, the public education system hands out condoms to minors.

The media's "war against drugs" has been replaced or followed by the "war against the tobacco industry." Drastic measures have been taken to reduce and prohibit smoking. Most American workplaces, public buildings, restaurants and commercial airlines now prohibit smoking. Through all of these "wars against such and such," where is the "war against alcohol?" If there is a sincere concern for youth, then why has this one isolated area also been (profitably) neglected? Are people not at all concerned with the excessive abuse of alcohol?

Today, college campuses across the United States are experiencing a new generation of alcoholism. Alcohol abuse breaks up marriages, causes infidelity, helps fuel young teens into premarital sex, and deadens the morality of all who partake in it. It is much more offensive in public than smoking is. A smoker does not get into a public brawl or kill or maim someone if he gets into an automobile. A smoker

---

[161]Ibid., pp. 58-59.

does not become abusive, disoriented, and mentally or emotionally impaired, and smoking does not kill brain cells. And finally, although smoking is a health hazard, it does not lead a person into becoming a destitute mental case or a street bum. Mixed messages like this, from the education system, media, and political domain, should make one feel only sympathy for the young people growing up under such misguided thinking.

In another way governmental laws in the U.S. have become intrusive. With the rise of social services and professionals, parents are told that if they spank their child that it is child abuse. This is a touchy subject because although there is a need to protect children from real physical or sexual abuse, these laws have done more harm than good from the perspective of most parents. Parents have lost control of their own children. Young children are learning toll-free numbers that will give them their local child protection agencies. What is a parent to do if "time out" does not work? To some this may sound as though one is asking for the license to beat their child, but this is not at all true. No parent wants to hurt his child, but sometimes a means of punishing a child does cross over into what could be defined as abuse. According to Child Welfare Services, "Physical abuse is generally defined as any non-accidental injury to the child and can include striking, kicking, burning, or biting the child, or any action that results in a physical impairment of the child."

The enemy is not progress. Progress, if done intelligently, does not mean families have to be forfeited. The real enemy is the manmade system, which arrogantly steams ahead disregarding the woman and closing man's mind to truth and religion.

# The Significance of Marriage and Child Care

Without a marriage institution and laws guiding relations between the sexes, just as without other laws, social life would be inconceivable. The need to control human behavior to some extent is obvious; otherwise, there would be anarchy and chaos. Sex is an internal part of the human personality; therefore, it cannot be denied, ignored or repressed. Nor can it be allowed to be expressed irresponsibly. In Western culture nearly everyone considers the uninhibited expression of their sexuality as a personal right. Indeed, Western men and women are completely free to have sexual relations in reckless, nonsensical ways. However, such activity is not only personally dangerous, it is a social problem that results in sexually transmitted diseases and creates illegitimate children. Most importantly from the social aspect, the availability of sex for single men and women outside of marriage causes the significance of the marriage institution to be greatly diminished.

The sexual drive in man is natural. Therefore, it must have a way of expression. It is such a strong drive that when it is repressed or allowed to run rampant, either condition will create serious repercussions, social disorder, and even psychic disturbances. Numerous child molestation and other sexual crime stories against youth by adult religious leaders, especially Catholic priests, makes one aware of the great strain a priest has been forced to endure. His vow of celibacy very often comes undone and is overtaken by the natural impulse he has as a human being, so long repressed. Thus, he is led away from his "moral" vow of celibacy and acts out in an "immoral" way with a juvenile.

Some celibates swore they were being sexually assaulted by seductive succubi (feminine demon spirits) while they slept. Among the sexually suppressed the intensity of such dreams or erotic hallucinations delve deep into the recesses of their oppressed bodies. "Pope Innocent VIII, Pope Benedict XIV, St. Augustine and St. Thomas, among other religious leaders, accepted the existence of incubi and succubi."[162]

The intimate, psychological gratification, the need for closeness, human touch, sense of security, and feelings of belonging are all intertwined with the act and meaning of relations between the sexes. Islam promotes sexual expression and does not think of either sex or marriage as sinful, but it promotes sexual expression only within the confines of marriage. Islam's stance on marriage is optimized by the saying of the Prophet (ﷺ):

> *"When a servant marries, he has completed half of his religion, so let him fear Allah concerning the remaining half."*[163]

Therefore, marriage is not only good for the individual and the society, but it is a moral and religious virtue for the Muslim.

## Islam's Preservation of the Individual, Marriage and Society

The beauty of Islam is realized when one sees how all of the components work together, complimenting one another. The very issues discussed thus far regarding Islam's stance on equality and the differences between men and women are of utmost importance because they are the major foundation upon which Muslims find their grounding. In addition to this, relations between men and women are valued in terms of comfort, purpose and necessity:

---

[162]*The Family Structure in Islam*, p. 51.
[163]Related by al-Bayhaqi – *hasan*.

*"They are clothing for you, and you are clothing for them."*[164]

A few contemporary misunderstandings about Islam, especially those regarding Muslim women, have already been mentioned. One Western writer claimed that Muslim women are treated inhumanely by their husbands. She said they are imprisoned, beaten and raped by them and lead lives of complete subjection to them. Such untruths cannot be dismissed or go unchallenged. Perhaps such accusations are just a way of promoting their own society, whose marital structure has all but collapsed. It seems such writings are a diversion of self-delusion in order to soothe their own sense of insecurity about the marital institute, which, as it is designed, is a most oppressive setup for women. The Western marriage system and divorce laws are being well protected by men in order to keep women in subjection.

The family is considered in Islam to be the most important foundation for a society. To neglect, abuse or degrade it would cause great concern because it is an institution decreed and endorsed by God:

*"O mankind, indeed We have created you from male and female and made you peoples and tribes that you may know one another. Indeed, the most noble of you in the sight of Allah is the most righteous of you. Indeed, Allah is Knowing and Acquainted."*[165]

The most important feature of the Islamic family is that it is ideally a solid, unified conglomerate of closeness where the members are codependent upon one another. All members care and feel responsible toward each other, and as a result, there are no feelings of isolation, abandonment or total independence.

---

[164] *Surah al-Baqarah*, 2:187.
[165] *Surah al-Hujurat*, 49:13.

In Islam the major goal of a mother is to raise her children within the guidance and values of their religion. By doing so, a mother cannot go wrong. Islam contains an enormous amount of positive guidance in all areas of life, including cleanliness, etiquette, sexuality, modesty, home life, economy, justice, finances, and more. It would be overwhelming if one were given all the rulings at one time. But as one grows in Islam, step by step, it is not experienced as such. Islam is not difficult to live by because its ordinances fit our nature. Islam places no burden too great on the individual, and the Qur'an confirms this:

*"But those who believed and did righteous deeds – We charge no soul except [within] its capacity."*[166]

## Building Nations

*"A man asked the Messenger of Allah (ﷺ) who among his near ones had the greatest right over him. The Prophet (ﷺ) replied, 'Your mother.' He asked, 'Then who is next?' The Prophet (ﷺ) replied, 'Your mother.' He again asked, 'Then who is next?' The Prophet (ﷺ) replied, 'Your mother.' He asked, 'Then who is next?' The Prophet (ﷺ) replied, 'Your father.'"*[167]

According to Islam, the most important role a woman performs during her lifetime is that of a mother. For this reason many Muslim women are very content to stay home and raise a family. Additionally, because they are being taken care of financially and since there is no negative social stigma related to being a mother, Muslim women do not feel they must prove their worth by doing additional work outside the home. This is not only a benefit for the woman but deters and prevents many social ills from taking root and

---

[166] *Surah al-A'raf,* 7:42.
[167] Related by al-Bukhari and Muslim.

spreading. When mothers stay home with their children, they are able to teach them true values as defined by Islam. Muslims are commanded in the Qur'an to worship and obey Allah first. After Allah, the ones who most deserve obedience, love and honor are parents.

The absence of the mother from the home can be seen in "latch-key kids," a Western term that has no place in an Islamic society. Latch-key kids go home to empty houses after school because both parents are at work. Employing someone to be with the children is expensive, so latch-key kids care for themselves until their parents return from work, usually for several hours. The society eventually bears the burden of these unsupervised, sometimes delinquent children. The statistics are alarming. "It is projected that 40% of American 14-year old girls will get pregnant by the time they are 19 years old. 135,000 high school students carry guns to school. Violent crimes committed by juveniles have more than doubled over the past five years. Six out of ten high school students say they have used illegal drugs."[168]

The problem is a serious one, especially when these children become older, more curious and exposed to more negative influences. Unsupervised kids, especially teens, get into trouble. Their trouble is directly related to the exorbitant amount of time they spend alone. They congregate with other kids who are in a similar situation. They find camaraderie and courage in numbers, so some youths form gangs. Many begin experimenting with marijuana and alcohol at alarmingly young ages, proof that there is a great void in their lives. Parenting today is lax and unobtrusive to kids. Delinquency among teens can only be blamed on the lack of parental supervision, intervention and control. Parents are mistaken if they think their children are going to

---

[168]Hal Mattern, "Good Values Vs. Bad Influences – Parents Rise to Task of Raising Kids with Spirit to Succeed in Today's World," *Arizona Republic,* September 5, 1993.

somehow learn correct moral, spiritual or ethical values from anywhere other than home.

# The Marriage Proposal

## Women in Islam

Muslim women gain their worth and equal standing with men through the practice of their religion. For a woman to be raised under the guidance of Islam is like a tiny grain of sand becoming a lustrous pearl, wedged safe inside a tough, impenetrable shell. The shell of Islam provides protection for the singular grain of sand and gives it a safe place of residence. Tightly secured within, the female is able to grow, undisturbed, and free from defect. Here there is no danger, no tide or waves to pull her away. Here there is peace. When it is time, she comes out a radiant, beautiful treasure – something to be admired, adored and protected from harm.

Teaching Muslim children the necessary values of Islam, of responsibility to God and society, modesty, chastity, family honor, and self-respect is the duty parents owe to their children in order for them to succeed in this life and in the life hereafter. The protection and guidance Islam offers both men and women is something very positive, especially when one is aware of what happens without it. As with all other aspects of Islamic life, marriage is unique in some ways, but for the most part it is simple and straightforward.

Due to the structure of the segregated society, Islamic marriages are often procured through the help and concern of family members and friends, who are approached by other relatives and friends when someone knows a man interested in getting married. In Islam there is no dating, as in Western cultures, so there are no date rape cases, no illegitimate pregnancies, and no hurried marital arrangements made. Until a Muslim man decides that he is ready for marriage, he does not intimately know women other than his own close family members, i.e., his mother, sisters and aunts. The same is true for Muslim women; they do not intimately know men other than their fathers, brothers and uncles. The father of the bride plays a great part in deciding whether or not a man is right for his daughter. If the father is not present or is deceased, the eldest brother then has the responsibility of getting to know the prospective husband's character to determine if he is a good Muslim or not. This is determined by questioning and investigating the man's family, friends, and work history. Once he has passed this initial and formal investigation, he is invited to meet the bride's family. Once his character and intentions are determined to be safe and viable (following the approval of both parties, which specifically includes the woman herself), a legal marriage is contracted.

In order to dispel the myth about the pre-Islamic pagan practice of arranged marriages where women or young girls had no right to consent to or reject a marriage proposal, according to Islamic law, the bride- and groom-to-be must both give their consent during all stages, or it will not be considered a lawful marriage. Therefore, both men and women have the right to reject any marriage proposal. A Muslim woman cannot be forced to marry without her consent. This was practiced only in an age when Muslims were ignorant of their religion. In addition, widowed and divorced women are free to remarry according to their own wishes after their prescribed waiting period.

Although the woman has full right to disagree to a union, her father also has the right to reject a proposed mate if he feels it will not be a good union. In the best interest of the daughter, the father may play a major role in determining who will be his son-in-law. The father or eldest brother acts as an intermediary for the Muslim woman. It must be added here that the way Islam bestows and fosters natural, caring, concerned feelings towards all relations can be seen in how the father or eldest brother assists the woman out of genuine care and not out of a desire to be a dictator. A good Muslim man is not one who throws his weight around but is one who is protective, sensible and loving. Most Muslim marriages are successful largely due to this single, yet important element of family interaction.

The treatment of wives in Islam is emphasized by the following *hadith*:

> *'A'ishah reported, "The Messenger of Allah* (ﷺ) *said, 'The best among you is he who is the most kind to his wife, and I am the kindest among you to my wives.'"*[169]

When talking about women, the Prophet (ﷺ) once referred to them as "glass vessels." Glass is a sturdy material, but it can be broken. The exhortations of good, gentle treatment towards women in the Qur'an and *hadith* are numerous. In another *hadith* the Prophet (ﷺ) told men not to treat women harshly or try to change their nature:

> *"Treat women kindly. Woman has been created from a rib, and the most crooked part of the rib is in the upper region. If you try to make it straight, you will break it; and if you leave it as it is, it will remain curved. So treat women kindly."*[170]

There are numerous other *hadith* and Qur'anic ordinances in regards to appropriate relations with women, teaching men how to relate to the opposite sex.

The marriage relationship in Islam is far from a mere contract, agreement or solemn covenant. Naturally, the gentle treatment of women in Islam is contrary to the many slanderous remarks made about Muslim men. Women who are brought up under Islamic guidance are not easily abused

---

[169]Related by at-Tirmidhi – *saheeh*.
[170]Related by al-Bukhari.

because they know how they should be treated. They will not tolerate anything else. Islam makes both men and women highly dignified, peaceful and serene members of society. Surely, those Muslim women who have been brought up in a peaceful Islamic country cannot have any idea how sheltered they have been from the cold, cruel realities of the world at large. They do not know what it is to be threatened by sexual harassment, rape, unfair legal systems, and the other injustices found in non-Islamic societies, where assaults on women take place at every turn.

Marriage is a commitment, and several considerations must be weighed beforehand. The Prophet (ﷺ) said:

> "*A man marries a woman for four reasons: for the sake of her wealth, her family chain, her beauty, or her love of religion. Marry one for her religiousness, and you will be blessed.*"[171]

In fact, man supplicates to God regarding his family:

> "***And those who say, 'Our Lord, grant us from among our wives and offspring comfort to our eyes and make us a leader [i.e., example] for the righteous.'***"[172]

Among the means of a Muslim woman's secure status are financial rights:

1. A Muslim woman is entitled to inherit from her father, mother, husband and children, and possibly other relatives under specific circumstances.

2. She is entitled to a *mahr* (dowry) from her husband, which is given at the time of marriage. This is obligatory, not optional, and no limit is set as to its amount. The *mahr* must be discussed between the husband and wife before marriage and be agreeable to

---

[171] Related by al-Bukhari and Muslim.
[172] *Surah al-Furqan,* 25:74.

both. Its amount is according to the financial means of the husband and the social status of the woman.

*"Give them their due compensation as an obligation. And there is no blame upon you for what you mutually agree to beyond the obligation. Indeed, Allah is ever Knowing and Wise."*[173]

3. Any money or property she owns or obtains from lawful sources belongs solely to her, and the husband cannot claim any share in them.
4. If she wishes, she can run her own business within the bounds of Islamic teachings. Again, the whole income is hers. Islamic law does not put any responsibility for domestic expenses on the woman.
5. In case of divorce she retains her *mahr* and all of her belongings, as well as the legal right to receive maintenance during the *'iddah* (waiting period). Exceptions are only applied in case of adultery.
6. If the husband dies, the wife's rights mentioned in the marriage contract have a priority in settlement of his property.[174]

"These rights have been granted by Islam to give a woman economic security within marriage and after its dissolution either by divorce or by the death of the husband."[175] Inheritance is laid out clearly in the Qur'an and must be followed strictly by all Muslims. All heirs are given an established amount from the estate of the deceased according to their status as wives, mothers, sons or daughters, etc.

The *mahr* given to the woman from the husband is an essential part of a Muslim marriage:

---

[173] *Surah an-Nisa'*, 4:24.
[174] Based upon *Women in Shariah*, p. 154.
[175] Ibid., p. 154.

> "And give the women [upon marriage] their [bridal] gifts graciously."[176]

The *mahr* should not be confused with the custom in some countries of giving a "bride-price," since marriage in Islam is not the sale of a bride to her husband. The *mahr* is distinctly different from the European dowry, which was given by the bride's father to the husband. The bride shared no part in it. This type of dowry was not unlike a bribe because many used it in order to marry off their daughters.[177] Conversely, the *mahr* received by the Muslim bride is hers exclusively.

## Companionship

Allah said to mankind regarding the marriage of two people:

> "And of His signs is that He created for you from yourselves mates that you may find tranquility in them; and He placed between you affection and mercy. Indeed in that are signs for a people who give thought."[178]

The idea of marriage in Islam is to unite two people in a strong bond and a challenging commitment. It is a commitment to life, society, and the dignified, meaningful survival and continuum of the human race. It is a righteous act and an act that demands great responsibility from both partners. According to Islam, marriage is a deed done out of obedience to Allah. Marriage is therefore among the most noble acts and means of human interaction. As the protectors and maintainers of women, Muslim husbands have many legal and financial burdens and responsibilities to their wives. This means that the Muslim woman cannot be forced to work or to contribute to her own maintenance, even

---

[176] *Surah an-Nisa'*, 4:4.
[177] *Women in Shariah*, p. 155.
[178] *Surah ar-Rum*, 30:21.

if she is rich.[179] Thus, the woman is freed to really spend time with her husband as a companion in the truest sense of the word. If she wants children, she has all the time to bring them up under her own guidance.

As a companion, the husband values her contributions and provides for his wife and children. As a father, he, too, must take on the demands of raising children. The father in Islam is the provider and a strong Muslim leader for his family. Children are expected to be respectful and obedient, and Islam demands that all people honor their parents:

> *"And your Lord has decreed that you not worship except Him, and to parents, good treatment. Whether one or both of them reach old age [while] with you, say not to them [so much as], 'uff,'[180] and do not repel them but speak to them a noble word."*[181]

Living Islamically might be described as living a less stressful and more simplified lifestyle. Within Islamic guidance women and men are freed to be together, know their roles, accept them, and find peace and happiness: the way Allah intended them to be. Their roles are defined, and there are no superior or subordinate personalities, nor are there any arrogant or subservient attitudes. Marriage from the Muslim woman's perspective is something good for her. She has companionship, protection, financial maintenance, and the ability to raise a family.

The Qur'an clearly commands men to be fair and rational with women, especially their wives. The Islamic *shari'ah* even prohibits men from obtaining a divorce during certain circumstances or situations in order to protect women and children from abuse and harsh separations. Thus, it is

---

[179] *The Family Structure in Islam,* p. 56.
[180] An expression of disapproval or irritation.
[181] *Surah al-Isra',* 17:23-24.

assured that Islam does not condone the cruel treatment of women to the slightest degree, even during the worst times of a marriage, i.e., when contemplating divorce. Any deviation from this principle cannot be considered true Islamic living.

## Leadership

According to Islam, one way in which a marriage resembles an organization or gathering of people who come together for a particular purpose is that within every gathering one person is expected to lead. The group is thus assured in case of a problem that there is someone who will take charge and has the degree of power to implement decisions. The most sophisticated organizations, such as the army, navy and police force, use a ranking method of authority. Those qualified occupy positions not only of power, but more importantly, positions where great responsibility has been designated. What would happen if there was not this system of authority in an operating room? What would happen if attendants started making the decisions and telling the surgeon what to do?

Islam made the husband the leader of the family because men are the protectors and maintainers of women:

> *"And due to them [i.e., the wives] is similar to what is expected of them, according to what is reasonable.*[182] *But the men have a degree over them [in responsibility and authority]. And Allah is Exalted in Might and Wise."*[183]

By this, more responsibility is placed upon the man. This Qur'anic injunction does not mean that men are lords over their wives and should not be taken out of context in any

---

[182] The wife has specific rights upon her husband, just as the husband has rights upon her.
[183] *Surah al-Baqarah,* 2:228.

other negative way. The husband is not to act arrogantly, abusively or like an authoritarian dictator. It is not as Westerners seem to assume – a master over the slave. If a husband were to act in such a manner, it would be an obvious breach of obedience and submission to Allah. Arrogance is not an Islamic trait. The Qur'an and *hadith* attest to that. Moreover, a Muslim woman is not under the subjection of her husband. Her first and only Lord is Allah. She expects only His reward when striving to please her husband in any good deed she may do. It is unlawful for a Muslim woman to obey her husband if he asked her to do anything contrary to what Islam expects from its believers. And, in much the same way, a husband would have grounds to exercise authority over his wife only if she acted out of the bounds of Islam.

By far, the biggest difference between Islamic and Western marriage is that in Islam the husband and wife do not run independently from one another. Women in the West come and go at all hours, and often their husbands do not even know where they are. And yet people are shocked when a woman is stalked, raped or even killed by some lunatic. Conclusively, it is not humanly possible to love someone and not feel protective of him/her.

Myths about Islam and Muslims are reminiscent of a Hollywood version of pre-Islamic Arabia where men act like vile creatures who abuse their many wives. But in reality, Islamic jurisprudence is emphatically very tough on all violent criminals. Muslim husbands are not immune either. They must treat their wives well and not cause them any physical harm or pain. Violence against women is not tolerated in Islam.

# Who Is Liberated in the West?

It is time to stop talking about women because the ones who have been liberated in the West do not wear dresses. If there is anyone who has won points from the Women's Liberation Movement, it certainly has got to be men. At every turn he leaps ahead, is promoted, is listened to in the workplace, and is catered to inside and outside of marriage, not only by the legal justice system and governmental politics, but also by the women of society. Feminists try to copy him, and this must make him feel even more superior. He has enjoyed up until now the best of both worlds. Certainly, the Western man lives in a "man's world" that has been described by some as a paradise for men.

## Is Paradise for Men Only?

One cannot predict how long this paradise will continue to thrive, but it is clear that if there should happen to be a real women's awakening and a real women's liberation movement, then its end would be easier to foresee. The Women's Movement has done nothing to change the way men and women live together as man and wife. In fact, it has created the type of society many men would crave: free sex, no marriage constraints, and no financial responsibilities. Most men applaud women's strides in the liberation movement because they know they are being let off the hook more and more as time goes by. Deep inside them they realize they would never trade places with a woman because her life is filled to the brim with extra familial demands, a lowered social status, and more stress.

What bothers most women about men in the West is that while they expect their wives to work outside, they still call housework "women's work." And then there is the man who makes his wife feel inferior by reminding her his salary is bigger than hers. In what way is this woman liberated when she is performing so much more than her share towards her relationship, marriage and family?

Only a few years ago women cleverly designed legally binding contracts called prenuptial agreements to protect their assets and economic security during marriage and in case of divorce. Men called women who asked for such contracts manipulative and demanding simply because they were looking out for themselves. If a woman has property, a high paying career or other assets, it becomes the partial property of her future husband if she does not state otherwise in a prenuptial agreement. This portrays the double standard women in the West face: whenever a man asserts himself or "beats the system," he is called intelligent and resourceful, but if a woman asserts herself, she is criticized and called manly or aggressive. The system is designed so that men are the only ones allowed to play.

## **Divorce in the West**

Unlike in Islam where the divorce process is not made public, divorce in the West is usually a humiliating experience, especially for women who have been out of work and raising a family. Sex discrimination exists even in the legal court processes and is a well-known, documented fact. Keeping in mind that most judges are male, women can bet on facing a prejudicial judgement in any type of court hearing. A 1993 National Association of Women Judges conference which discussed sexism found that "judges favored husbands in the distribution of marriage assets because they don't consider housework as work. Judges viewed female attorneys less credibly than male attorneys. Male litigants received higher personal injury awards than female litigants. Female minors received harsher sentences than male minors."[184]

---

[184] *Women Pay More (and How to Put a Stop to It)*, p. 126.

An example of how this discrimination thrives can be seen in a non-contested divorce hearing regarding the joint custody of a child in 1991. The father had a four-year college degree and was earning much more than the woman, so they decided that the father would take the child on weekdays and the mother on weekends. Other expenses such as doctor bills would be split 40-60, the father paying 60%. At the court hearing the judge looked over their plan and confronted the woman, who was without legal representation. He calmly told her he thought that she could pay the father perhaps fifty to one-hundred dollars per month.

The legal ramifications of divorce invariably favor men. If a father takes custody of the children, the Western public considers him a saint. Concurrently, if the woman willingly gives custody to the father, she is stigmatized because she is going out of the norms of society. Women experience divorce far differently than the way men do. Men who have divorced often describe the lifting of a great burden, but women face additional stress. Research has shown significant lifestyle changes for both the husband and wife after divorcing. Very often the man's standard of lifestyle improves by at least 30%, while the woman's typically drops dramatically, especially if she does not have a college education, has been out of work, or has been a mom at home. For most women holding traditional jobs, divorce means their financial status can easily go below the poverty level.

## Children Without Fathers

Today more than ever, victims of a free society are the children. With 15 million children in the United States living in poverty, it is not difficult to understand the stresses and injustices being faced. It can be safely assumed that for the most part, these children are living with their single mothers, who are usually earning much less than the fathers. The term used for those fathers who after divorce make a complete disappearing act, do not pay child support, and who carry on as if they never had a child is "deadbeat dads." Contemporary studies show how important the father figure is for all children. Boys, especially, need a male role figure to learn from. This is not to say that mothers are not good role models, but current studies are showing a disadvantage for children raised without their fathers. Without the father's presence, researchers contend, children are more likely going to learn how to deal with life much the same way their mothers do, often more emotionally charged. Boys raised in the absence of a father are especially able to manipulate the mother who is not as rigid in discipline as a father usually is. Before long the kids are out from under the mother's control.

There have been studies documenting that 98% of juvenile offenders come from homes with absent fathers or homes with stepfathers, while in contrast, only 17% were without a mother. While there are numerous studies linking a mother's absence due to working outside of the home, there seems to be a correlation that has been ignored between delinquency and weak or absent fathers.[185] As Terri Apter puts it, "Sons need fathers if they are to mature into adults who can function in this demanding and often unfriendly society."[186] Men who have had the benefit of a strong bond with their fathers are most likely to be successful in their education and careers; they are less emotional and more logical in their approach to life. Because men show more interest in studies about automobiles, electronics and architecture, they often know how to deal more effectively with things related to everyday necessities, such as the maintenance of automobiles and house repairs. These little

---

[185] *Working Women Don't Have Wives – Professional Success in the 1990s,* pp. 98-99.
[186] Ibid., p. 99.

but valuable how-to techniques are of vital importance to everyday living. Without a man around the house women find they struggle more with things they do not fully understand or have an interest in.

New studies suggest that even young girls are deeply affected when raised without a father. In short, the studies found that women who had a strong father figure were more likely to succeed in the social stratosphere in comparison to women who did not grow up with fathers.

## Divorce in Islam

> *"And if you fear dissension between the two, send an arbitrator from his people and an arbitrator from her people. If they both desire reconciliation, Allah will cause it between them."*[187]

Devout Muslims take their marriages seriously because in Islam divorce is disliked and should be considered the very last resort for a bad or strained relationship. If problems arise in a marriage, both parties should try to obtain help through the channels of family intervention. Divorce in Islam is vastly different from the Western divorce procedure, mainly because its laws are well defined and unchangeable, yet easy and just. It is highly beneficial when the laws of the land remain the same. For this reason Muslims have a great advantage if they live in an Islamic society. They know what to expect both in cases of marriage and divorce. The West does not have such a beneficial system. There it is a game of chance. One has to hire an expensive attorney and hope to get an unbiased judge. Constantly changing laws can raise havoc too.

In Islam divorce is forbidden under certain circumstances. It is legally forbidden to pronounce divorce

---

[187] *Surah an-Nisa'*, 4:35.

during a woman's monthly cycle and if the couple has had intercourse after her last monthly period. This prohibition addresses a few pertinent matters for all involved. For one, a woman is likely to experience emotional ups and downs during menstruation. This in turn creates more stress and may deter a reconciliation. If divorce is presented to a woman during this time, she may tend to be more emotional, which could cause undue trauma for her and her family. After the pronouncement of divorce an additional waiting period of three monthly cycles must pass in order to facilitate any possible reconciliation. If the woman is pregnant, the waiting time is until the birth of the baby, regardless of the length of time. The Muslim man, regardless of his desire for divorce at this time, must wait out the entire period of pregnancy. In other words, he cannot abandon his wife while she is carrying their child. He must continue to maintain her throughout the pregnancy, and possibly after the birth of their child when divorce is final. The mother can nurse her child and thus receive support from its father until it reaches the age of two. Should the mother refuse, the husband must be prepared to hire someone else as a nurse.[188]

The waiting period as prescribed acts as a buffer. Divorce is stressful enough for all concerned. The waiting period is often a time for reconciliation, which is permissible and even desirable. Whatever the circumstance, Islam forbids cruel treatment of either partner, and equitable, humane respect is expected from every person involved.

Islamic divorce does not take place publicly in front of a judge[189] or courtroom full of strangers. God-consciousness is a fundamental underlying force in Islam; therefore, Muslim men and women are expected to be responsible at all times, even during the delicate process of divorce. Due to

---

[188] *The Family Structure in Islam,* p. 246.
[189] A legal judge who is a scholar of *shari'ah* is only obtained when a woman is seeking the divorce.

the element of religious and moral uprightness required of Muslims and because Islam has defined everything, making a divorce public would not be beneficial.

In Islam the general grounds for divorce are simple and humane. It is the inability of either the husband or wife to continue keeping their marital duties. It might be that one simply cannot live peacefully or compassionately with the other. It is inhumane to force a person to stay with someone under duress. Some acceptable reasons to justify a wife's request for divorce would be an extended period of the husband's absence from his wife without her consent. Another reason might be that the husband neglects or stops providing for his wife, excessive financial stress, or the inability to physically father children.[190] Circumstances which require dissolution are when a wife accepts Islam but the husband does not or when either partner denounces his/her faith. Also, if the marriage contract is found to be incorrect or void due to falsification or error, a divorce must take place.[191]

During the waiting period (*'iddah*) prior to a divorce being finalized, the woman is entitled to full maintenance. She has the right to stay in her home and cannot be expelled. She must be treated fairly:[192]

> *"O Prophet, when you [Muslims] divorce women, divorce them for [the commencement of] their waiting period and keep count of the waiting period, and fear Allah, your Lord. Do not turn them out of their [husbands'] houses, nor should they [themselves] leave [during that period] unless they are committing a clear immorality. And those are the limits [set by]*

---

[190]*The Family Structure in Islam,* p. 225.
[191]Ibid., p. 226.
[192]Ibid., p. 246.

Allah. And whoever transgresses the limits of Allah has certainly wronged himself."[193]

The divorce is final after the waiting period is finished. The couple may now go their separate ways. For children under the age of two, the mother is given custody for the purpose of breastfeeding.[194] The father is at this time required to pay for the maintenance of the mother and child until the child reaches the age of weaning:

> "Mothers may nurse [i.e., breastfeed] their children two complete years for whoever wishes to complete the nursing [period]. Upon the father is their [i.e., the mothers'] provision and their clothing according to what is reasonable. No person is charged with more than his capacity. No mother should be harmed through her child, and no father through his child."[195]

If no agreement is reached by the parents concerning custody, the child is normally retained by the mother during preschool years and then may be given to the father, unless it is against the best interests of the child.

It must be understood that Muslim men are forever the wards and providers for their children even after divorce. This means that children in Islam are protected by this command, unlike in the West where "deadbeat dads" exist. If the father is granted custody, he cannot forbid the mother from seeing, keeping contact or visiting her children. This is anti-Islamic and would be cruel. In Islam, divorce does not mean the end of the parent-child relationship. One of the prerequisites of entrance to Heaven is that one has been good to and has honored the womb which bore him.

---

[193] *Surah at-Talaq*, 65:1.
[194] *The Family Structure in Islam*, p. 246.
[195] *Surah al-Baqarah*, 2:233.

A couple may be divorced twice, after which they may remarry. However, after the third divorce it is forbidden to reconcile until the woman has first married another man with the intention of permanence. Then she must have been widowed or divorced from the second husband. This forces couples to be very careful about their actions and words towards one another and does not allow for the ease of divorce to be abused or taken for granted. Divorce in Islam has been made easy, but not so easy that people will take advantage of it.

# Conclusion

In Western culture too many people are suffering economically, emotionally and spiritually. More importantly, this suffering is giving birth to ever-widening social ills that will persist and only spell doom in future days unless the wake-up calls are heeded and lifestyles and philosophies reevaluated. The false sense of personal freedom that has much of the world's population on a crash course with disaster is nothing more than human enslavement cloaked in tantalizing forms.

Islam holds the key that will unlock the door to human liberation at all levels. Not all is doom. There is hope. The damage women have done themselves through their self-proclaimed prophets of liberation/feminism can be repaired. Current pop-philosophies aside, the mandates and guidelines for achieving true freedom have already been revealed and only wait for human beings to reflect upon them and act accordingly.

Ultimately, the only way women will obtain their true standing in life is through a return to religion, because religion is the only natural source which requires mankind to revere women and the wombs which bore them. As modern civilization takes man on a spiritless venture away from religion, this truth will become increasingly manifest.

A few of the truths of Islam found in the Qur'an and authentic *hadith* have been presented with the intent to share, educate, and enlighten. The previous discourse was presented by comparison to show the alternative ways of life. While Islam grants women equality with men, it does not imply in any way that women and men are the same. Within Islam is the guide to true "feminism" because there is no competition between the sexes or game playing, and abusive practices are not tolerated. Islam grants to women their natural place in life, and through this process they find happiness, liberation and peace.

# Bibliography

Abdalati, Hammudah, *Islam in Focus,* revised ed., Saudi Arabia: Abul-Qasim Publishing House, 1993.

Abd al Ati, Hammudah, *The Family Structure in Islam,* Indiana: The American Trust Publications, 1977.

Apter, Terri, *Working Women Don't Have Wives – Professional Success in the 1990s,* New York: St. Martin's Press, 1994.

Badawi, Dr. Jamal, *The Status of Woman in Islam,* reprint of essay found in quarterly journal, *Al-Ittihad,* vol. 8, no. 2, 1971, The Muslim Students Association of the U.S. and Canada, 1980.

Bagdikian, B., *The Media Monopoly,* 4th ed., Boston: Beacon Press, 1992.

Bloom, Allan, Prof., *The Closing of the American Mind,* foreword by Saul Bellow, 1st ed., New York: Simon & Schuster, 1988.

Boris, Eileen, *Home to Work – Motherhood and the Politics of Industrial Homework in the United States,* Melbourne: Cambridge University Press, 1994.

Doi, Abdur Rahman, *Women in Shariah,* 3rd ed., Kuala Lumpur: A.S. Noordeen, 1990.

Faludi, Susan, *Backlash – The Undeclared War Against the American Women,* New York: Doubleday, 1991.

Izetbegovic, Alija, *Islam Between East and West,* 2nd ed., Indiana: American Trust Publications, 1991.

al-Kanadi, Abu Bilal Mustafa, *The Islamic Ruling Regarding Women's Dress According to the Quran and Sunnah,* Jeddah, Saudi Arabia: Abul-Qasim Publishing House, 1991.

Limbaugh, Rush, *The Way Things Ought to Be,* New York: Pocket Books, Simon & Schuster, 1993.

Morris, William, ed., *American Heritage Dictionary of the English Language,* Boston: Houghton Mifflin Co., 1981.

Paglia, Camille, et al., *Sexual Harassment – Confrontations and Decisions,* edited by Edmund Wall, New York: Prometheus Books, 1992.

Qutb, Sayyid, *Milestones,* Beirut, Lebanon: The Holy Koran Publishing House, 1978.

Seldes, George, *The Great Thoughts,* foreword by Henry Steele Commager, New York: Ballantine Books, 1985.

Saheeh International, *The Qur'ān: English Meanings and Notes,* Riyadh: Al-Muntada al-Islami Trust, 2001-2012; Jeddah, Dar Abul-Qasim, 1997-2001.

Weeks, Jeffrey, *Sexuality,* England: Ellis Horwood Limited, 1986.

Whittelsey, Frances and Marcia Carroll, *Women Pay More (and How to Put a Stop to It),* introduction by Ralph Nader, New York: The New Press, 1995.